MINISTRY

It's Not Just for Ministers

GARY MORSCH
EDDY HALL

Beacon Hill Press of Kansas City
Kansas City, Missouri

To the 40-some ministers,
both professional and lay,
at the First Church of the Nazarene of Newton, Kans.,
who helped bring this book to life.

CONTENTS

FOREWORD

A layperson said to me at a church workday activity one Saturday, "Well, Pastor, what are you going to preach tomorrow—the usual message, 'Pray more and work harder'?" I was caught red-handed—and red-faced!

He was right. So much preaching is simply an exhortation for laypersons to do the same thing—only harder.

Not this book. Here is a clear call for the laity to adopt a new way of thinking. Ministry is not just for the clergy. In fact, it is primarily for the laity.

In the book that launched the American church growth movement, *Your Church Can Grow,* C. Peter Wagner stated, "Growing churches, whether they be large or small, know how to motivate their laypeople, how to create structures which permit them to be active and productive, and how to guide them into meaningful avenues of Christian service."[1]

Every follower of Jesus is called to serve the Kingdom according to his or her spiritual gifts and degree of skillfulness. The laity are responsible for more than menial tasks around the church. They are "full partners" in the work of ministry.

Equal lay and clergy representation in the government of the Church of the Nazarene is legendary. It is time for *equality in ministry* to be extended to the laity too!

This book is a road map to help laypersons become

more intensively engaged in fulfilling the Great Commission. The task is so enormous, so demanding, so promising that every Christian is needed—and privileged—to be involved.

> *Rise up, O [people] of God!*
> *Have done with lesser things;*
> *Give heart and mind and soul and strength*
> *To serve the King of Kings.*
>
> —William Pierson Merrill

—BILL M. SULLIVAN
Church Growth Division
Church of the Nazarene

PREFACE

In Matt. 9:36-38 we are viewing the great need of humanity through the eyes of Jesus as it reads, "But when he saw the multitudes, he was moved with compassion on them, because they fainted, and were scattered abroad, as sheep having no shepherd. Then saith he unto his disciples, The harvest truly is plenteous, but the labourers are few; pray ye therefore the Lord of the harvest, that he will send forth labourers into his harvest" (KJV).

Jesus calls attention to the "harvest," the great mass of humanity who are scattered, broken, and lost. It is always harvesttime somewhere in our world, and the challenge is ever before us. Jesus gives the imperative of prayer. Great spiritual events and movements are founded on intercessory prayer.

The question is not "Do we pray enough?" The question is "Do we pray at all?" *Intercessory* prayer is weeping over the harvest and praying for laborers to go into the fields. For some unknown reason we have limited the application of the term "harvester" to pastors, missionaries, or evangelists and have forgotten that the great commission of Christ appeals to every Christian to be a witness and to enter into the harvest.

Gary Morsch, as a Christian physician, has caught the New Testament truth that every believer should be a soul winner. He writes, "I am convinced that an essential part [in growing churches] is that . . . the laypeople are full partners in ministry. They don't expect the pastor and staff to do the work of ministry for them." He not only has caught the vision of the vital role of the total Body of Christ being in ministry but also is involved in both local and international ministries of compassion and evangelism.

This is more than a high ideal or a nonrealistic theory. It is a biblical challenge with real methods and plans of action.

The population is too large for only ordained ministers to reach the world. It is now the call of Christ to every believer to be "light and salt" to a desperate world.

—WILLIAM J. PRINCE
General Superintendent
Church of the Nazarene

ACKNOWLEDGMENTS

We started work on this book with high hopes. It would be alive with compelling stories of real, ordinary laypeople involved in life-changing ministry. It would be fun, even exciting to read, and above all it would present practical truths about lay ministry in simple, powerful ways so that you could easily understand and apply them.

Once our outlining, research, and interviewing were done, but before much actual writing had taken place, that dream seemed in jeopardy. How could we be sure we were speaking to the real needs people felt, not just harping on our own pet themes? Were we overlooking important issues that thousands of Nazarene laypeople would want to see addressed? Would the learning activities in the leader's guide really work in class sessions as they were intended?

That's when Eddy called Pastor Larry Morgan at First Church of the Nazarene in Newton, Kans., and asked, "Do you have a group in your congregation who would be willing to participate in a pilot study of a new book on ministry for laypeople?" We couldn't have asked for a more cooperative or enthusiastic pastor. A study on this topic, he said, seemed to be perfectly timed in terms of what God was already doing in the church.

Larry announced the study to his congregation, and about 30 people signed up. For each of the five Sunday afternoons in January 1993, 20 to 30 laypeople met to explore the key concepts of this book together.

Once that group started meeting, there was no longer anything theoretical about writing the book. These were real people who intensely wanted to be used more effectively in ministry, and they had real questions. They described with amazing transparency both their hopes for ministry as well as their frustrations. They responded to the teaching sometimes with enthusiasm for how helpful it was, and at other times by pointing out how a poorly written story distracted them from what it was intended to teach. Some teaching methods proved amazingly effective; others had to be changed because they didn't work as planned.

By the fifth week more than 40 people had taken part in the class. At the close of the final session, the group members stood in a circle, held hands, and thanked God for the powerful way their visions for ministry had been broadened and how some had begun to more clearly understand their gifts and callings.

Much of the passion and urgency you'll find in these pages, as well as a good deal of the clarity, is thanks to that group. Whatever ministry this book has, they share in it.

The other group who make this book what it is are those who told us their stories. Many of those stories made it into print, while many others did not, for lack of space or other reasons. But all contributed to making this a better book by giving us a pool of excellent stories to draw from and by making it possible for us to use those best suited to our teaching goals.

Veteran editors Steve Miller and James N. Watkins graciously agreed to read the manuscript and offered many valuable suggestions to make the book more readable, interesting, and accurate.

Our thanks to Bonnie Perry of Nazarene Communications and to the staff of Nazarene Publishing House, who extended us extraordinary grace on our deadline (made necessary because of our late start on the project), yet still managed to publish the book in time for the 1993 Nazarene General Assembly in Indianapolis.

This book would never have been written had it not been for the vision of Dr. Bill Sullivan, executive director of the Church Growth Division of the Church of the Nazarene, who so believed in its message that his division sponsored it, providing funds for its writing and guaranteeing its enthusiastic promotion.

Most of all we thank God, whose guidance and provision has been evident throughout the project, bringing together the right people at just the right time and providing extraordinary strength when the load of the work threatened to overwhelm. We now offer the book back to Him to be used for His glory.

INTRODUCTION

An Exciting Time to Serve God

I (Gary) believe we are entering one of the most exciting eras in the history of the Church of the Nazarene. Many are calling it a movement. Some call it a revolution. But whatever you call it, I believe it is going to explode within the next few years, ushering in a period of phenomenal ministry and growth.

What is this movement, this revolution? It is the rediscovery and renewal of the ministry of the laity.

The ministry of the laity is nothing new. It is as old as the gospel itself. The New Testament Church was a great example of the ministry of all believers. While different believers had different ministries, each Christian was expected to use his or her spiritual gifts for ministry, and the Church flourished, spreading throughout the world.

In time, though, ministry became professionalized. The nonprofessionals, or laity, were relegated to a second-class status that all but locked them out of recognized ministry. This division of believers into two classes—"ministers" and "nonministers"—persisted stubbornly through the centuries. From time to time spiritual leaders such as Martin Luther attacked this heresy, and with some success. But it is only in our day, I believe, that the full harvest of their efforts in this area will be reaped.

Through my volunteer work with Compassionate Ministries I have had the privilege of meeting thousands of Nazarenes in many countries. I have found it exciting to witness the tremendous growth of so many of our churches. Often I have noticed that churches outside North America are growing faster than most of those within. What, I have wondered, makes the difference in them? Why are they growing so fast?

An essential part of the answer, I am convinced, is that in these churches the laypeople are full partners in ministry. They don't expect the pastor and staff to do the work of ministry for them. It is primarily the laypeople, supported by their pastors, who are reaching out and winning their communities for Christ. In many cases, in fact, it is laypeople who are planting the new churches.

I believe the unleashing of the laity that is now taking place, not only in the Church of the Nazarene but also in a great many other denominations throughout the world, has the potential to impact our communities and our world for Christ in ways few if any of us can imagine. As the number of believers saying yes to God's call to minister multiplies, and as the Church equips and supports its members in fulfilling their calls, the Church's effectiveness in fulfilling its mission is also multiplying.

Many believe the Church of the Nazarene is approaching a critical point in its history. Will we be ready for the challenges of the future?

I believe we will.

We will be ready because of denominational leaders who are committed to empowering laypeople to find and fulfill their ministries in the church and in the world. We will be ready because of the many pastors who are claiming and fulfilling their biblical role of equipping believers for ministry. We will be ready because of the great host of laypeople who even now are being called out by God to dedicate their lives to ministry. And we will be ready because God has ordained that His Church will be built by a great ministry partnership of all believers.

What an exciting time this is to serve God! What an exciting day to be called into ministry!

Over the centuries millions of Christians have believed a crippling myth: "Ministry is just for 'ministers.'" God's call to ministry, so the myth goes, comes only to the select few. The rest of us are laypeople by default, called only to receive ministry and support the ministries of others.

But the Bible renounces this myth with an empowering truth: If I am a Christian, I am called to minister.

1

THE MINISTRY MYTH

When I (Gary) was 10 years old, this business of ministry all seemed so simple.

As I listened to a sermon about being open to God's call to ministry, I believed God was calling me. That morning I knelt and dedicated my life to whatever ministry God would call me to. Then I stood and announced, "God has called me to be a minister!"

In the months that followed, hardly a Wednesday night prayer meeting went by that I did not stand and testify, "God has called me to be a minister." Afterward, supportive church members would encourage me. "You'll make a fine preacher, just like your daddy," they would say.

Then several months later, in another service, I once again felt God talking to me about my future. I did not hear an audible voice, but just as surely as I had earlier sensed that God wanted me to commit my life to ministry, I felt God was impressing on me that I was to work in the field of science.

I was confused. Did God call people to be more than one thing? How could I be both a minister and a scientist?

I took my confusion to my dad. "Dad, can a person be a minister and a scientist at the same time?"

Inasmuch as the Bible nowhere uses the word *minister(s)* to refer exclusively to ministry professional(s), where it is used in that sense in this book it is placed in quotation marks.

Dad thought for a while, then responded, "Sure."

"What do they call someone who is both a minister and a scientist?"

"Well, let's see," Dad said. "I guess you would say God has called you to be a research minister."

I had no clue what a "research minister" was, but it sounded good, so for many more months on Wednesday nights I testified that God had called me to be a research minister. (It could have been worse—my dad could have said God was calling me to be a "Christian scientist.") I repeated the testimony until an older Christian friend advised me there really was no such thing as a research minister and pointed out that God surely intended for me to go into "the ministry."

Never again would I stand on a Wednesday night and testify that God had called me into ministry. Though the sense of call to ministry was as strong as ever, I had painfully learned that to mention that call publicly was to invite pressure from others to enter "the ministry"—to be a pastor, evangelist, or missionary. I did not believe God was calling me to be any of those, but I couldn't explain to anyone else—or even to myself—how that could be true if God had in fact called me to be a minister. Rather than raise questions I could not answer, I just quit talking to other people about my call.

I had long assumed that after graduation from high school I would go on to a Nazarene college. But when graduation time came, I found my inner battle over God's call was paralyzing me. How could I go to college if I was confused about what God was leading me to do? How would I know how to prepare? Maybe I was mistaken, and God really was calling me to be a pastor, missionary, or evangelist. But in my heart I knew I was not mistaken. God had called me to be a minister, but in some other way—some way I had not yet been able to imagine.

The turmoil over my calling led me to do something untypical for a good Christian kid who was supposed to be enrolling in a Nazarene college: I joined the army. It seemed an unlikely choice. It was 1969, the Vietnam War was going strong, thousands of soldiers were dying, and 17-year-olds had to have their parents' permission to be sent off to war. But God can use anything, and He used my time in the military to begin showing me that I could minister without being in the professional ministry.

Wherever I was stationed, I always became as involved as possible in the local Nazarene church, teaching Sunday School or working with the youth group. While stationed at Fort Benning, Ga., I even served as supply pastor for the Macon Church of the Nazarene. Though I did not fully realize it at the time, God was beginning to show me that being a layperson did not keep me from being a minister. I came out of the army ready to attend college and prepare for the ministry—as a layperson.

I was beginning to understand that the confusion I had labored under for years was all because of believing what I now call the ministry myth: "Ministry is just for 'ministers.'" And "ministers," of course, meant only full-time ministry professionals.

Though I didn't know what field God wanted me to enter, I did know I was going to college to prepare for ministry. So without declaring myself a religion major, I started taking religion courses while waiting for God to make His direction clear.

But on campus I found the ministry myth alive and well. Time and again I was subtly reminded by well-meaning students and faculty members that a Christian serves God best as a ministry professional, not as a layperson. Chapel speakers often challenged us to say yes to God's call to full-time professional ministry, but rarely did any challenge us to respond to God's call to ministry as laypeople.

I gave God every opportunity to call me into full-time professional ministry. That is what everyone else seemed to expect, and I too had come to expect it. But the call to be a pastor or missionary never came.

During a time of prayer and reflection in my junior year, I was searching for God's will for the future. More than ever I sensed God's call to ministry, but I was also feeling impressed to change my major to premedicine. That was a surprise. It was the one thing I had secretly longed to do, but I had never seriously considered it because the ministry myth had convinced me that medicine was not real ministry. God made clear to me that day, however, that I was to minister through medicine. This call was confirmed when my pastor said, "As a doctor, you will have opportunities to minister to all kinds of people in the community that I will never be able to reach as a pastor." And so I spent the rest of my schooling preparing for ministry as a medical doctor.

The high cost of the myth

I wish my experience was unique, but as I talk with other laypeople, I am often reminded it's not. The ministry myth has been so widely believed for so long that it has no doubt kept millions of Christians from seeing themselves as ministers and recognizing what God was calling them to do. While this myth has paralyzed many in this way, it has crippled the ministries of others by causing them to misinterpret God's call.

My friend Mark knew that laypeople could minister, but he bought into the version of the ministry myth that says, "God can best use those who are in the professional ministry." Wanting to invest his whole life in ministry so that he could be as effective as possible for the kingdom of God, he quit his job, invested three years in a seminary education, then joined a church staff.

In his new position Mark was responsible to equip people for ministry and provide administrative support for the ministry of others. While he enjoyed much of the work, he quickly discovered that his gift wasn't administration. "I'm most effective in one-on-one ministry," he said. "And rather than coordinating existing ministries, I'd much rather be bringing new people in. I'd thought joining a church staff would give me more time for such things, but in fact it limited the time I could spend doing what I did best."

Mark resigned his church staff job, even though he knew some would misunderstand. "A lot of people might think that having served on a church staff and now being in the insurance business, I've settled for 'God's second best,'" he said. "But I now have far more opportunity for the ministry God has called me to as an insurance agent than I ever had on church staff.

"The passion of my life is to offer God's hope to broken people. Though I didn't realize it when I went into insurance, it is a perfect job for someone who wants to work with hurting people. Whenever an elderly client loses a spouse, I get a phone call. When any of my clients divorce, they have to come to me to change their insurance papers. And, of course, whenever one of them has a car accident, a fire, or a serious illness covered by a policy I carry, the client comes to see me.

"My work gives me lots of opportunities to sit down and talk with people in crisis. Most of them don't know Christ, and I often have the chance to share with them the Source of my hope. Just a few weeks ago I told my wife, 'I've never before felt God using me in ministry like I have lately.'"

The ministry myth led Mark into a professional ministry position for which he was not gifted and which actually limited his contact with the people to whom God was calling him to minister. It was only when he understood that God could use him more effectively as a layperson than as a professional minister that God was able to put Mark's ministry gifts to fullest use.

Where did the myth come from?

For centuries much of the church has divided itself into two groups—the clergy, or "ministers," and the laity, the ones ministered to. Where did this historic division within the church come from? Does it find its roots in Scripture?

Not at all. The New Testament clearly teaches that God has given every Christian one or more spiritual gifts with which to minister. Paul wrote the Corinthians, "There are different kinds of gifts, but the same Spirit. . . . to each one the manifestation of the Spirit is given for the common good" (1 Cor. 12:4, 7). Peter wrote, "Serve one another with whatever gift each of you has received" (1 Pet. 4:10, NRSV). Though in the Old Testament only a select group of God's people served as priests, in the New Testament Church all believers are priests—mediators between God and the rest of the people (2:5, 9). We are all called to offer God's love and forgiveness to other people and to bring their needs and concerns to God.

One pastor writes, "There is no room in the New Testament church for a hierarchy of callings. There is no biblical or theological justification for regarding church leaders as peculiarly called of God to minister holy things or to be 'full-time' for God, while considering the layperson, who serves God in both church and world, as having a lesser call or no call at all. The call of God comes to every believer who has ears to hear."[1]

God does call certain people to roles of leadership in the Church, but in describing their call, Scripture does not single them out as "the ministers." Rather, it emphasizes the ministry of *all* believers: "The gifts he gave were that some would be apostles, some prophets, some evangelists, some pastors and teachers, *to equip the saints for the work of ministry*" (Eph. 4:11-12, NRSV, emphasis added). The call of church leaders, then, is not to do the work of ministry so that we don't have to, but to equip *us* to do ministry.

Gordon Cosby, pastor of the Church of the Saviour in Washington, D.C., says it this way: "The primary task of the professional minister [is] training nonprofessional ministers for their ministry."[2]

Although the New Testament teaches that all believers are ministers, over the centuries a separation between "ministers" (clergy) and "nonministers" (laity) developed and widened. A fourth-century church document stated that the laity should merely "sit and say amen."[3] In 619 a church council ruled that the laity and clergy should remain separate. They based their ruling on Deut. 22:10, which states that "an ox and a donkey" should not plow together.[4]

Throughout history there have been many attempts to correct this unbiblical division. Of these, the Protestant Reformation, sparked in 1517 when Martin Luther posted his 95 Theses on a church door, is the best known. In reaffirming "the priesthood of all believers," Luther had simply rediscovered a biblical truth, that God has "made us to be . . . priests" (Rev. 1:6).

A few centuries later John Wesley founded a movement that would ultimately give birth to the Church of the Nazarene. His controversial practice of appointing and training hundreds of laymen to be preachers was doubtless a major reason for the movement's widespread impact.

Signs of hope

The fact that today we are still needing to talk about reclaiming ministry for all believers shows that the work of the Reformation is not yet complete. But there are signs of hope.

Almost 1,800 years ago, Tertullian, one of the Early Church fathers, said that baptism could be regarded as the ordination of the laity. Recently, Gordon Wetmore, president of Nazarene Theological Seminary, echoed that thought when he said that laypeople are as much ordained by God into the ministry as anyone else.

More and more Christians are realizing that we are all called to minister. People who have never before seen themselves as ministers are now saying, "Yes, I am a minister." One clergyman has written that the notion that all ministry is done by the pastors is "as dead as last year's bird's nest."[5]

This may be a bit optimistic, but even if the myth that "ministry is just for 'ministers'" is not quite dead, it clearly is dying. In recent years we have seen more and more laity returning to the ministry. Pastors are reclaiming their biblical role of equipping believers for ministry. Because they know the Church can never fulfill its mission as long as only a handful of leaders do the work, they are trying to mobilize every believer in their churches. As laypeople embrace their calls to minister and pastors give priority to equipping them for ministry, we are all learning to work together as ministry partners in new and creative ways.

It is only as we recognize that each of us is called to minister and as each of us says yes to that call that the church can fulfill its mission to be the hands and feet of Christ in a hurting world.

*"Ministry in its purest and simplest form
is love. . . . Ministry is, in fact, doing love!"*
—Win Arn
Church growth movement leader

2

WASHING DIRTY FEET

It was a holy moment. Jesus had just offered His disciples the bread, representing His body, and the cup, representing His blood, instituting the Lord's Supper. It was His last meal with His disciples before His death. He would soon be taken from them.

And what did the disciples do? They argued. "A dispute arose among them as to which of them was considered to be greatest" (Luke 22:24).

Probably in response to this dispute, Jesus silently rose from the table, took off His robe, and wrapped a towel around His waist, taking on the appearance of a slave. "After that, he poured water into a basin and began to wash his disciples' feet, drying them with the towel that was wrapped around him" (John 13:5).

The roads of Palestine were dusty in dry weather and muddy when it was wet. The sandals most people wore offered little protection against dust and mud. So by the door of each house stood a large waterpot, and as guests came in, a servant would meet them with a pitcher and towel to wash their feet.

Since Jesus and His disciples had no servant, they must have normally shared this duty among themselves. But this night, perhaps because of the competitive spirit among them, no one had washed feet—until Jesus rose to do it.

When He had finished, Jesus put His robe back on, again taking on the appearance of the rabbi, and returned to His place. "Now that I, your Lord and Teacher, have washed your feet," He said, "you also should wash one another's feet" (John 13:14).

Those words still call to us across the centuries. Not only does God call us to address spiritual needs (the ministry of the rabbi), but also He calls us to meet even the simplest of physical needs—needs others may consider unworthy of their personal attention (the ministry of the servant). To follow Jesus is to minister to both kinds of needs.

What needs does love care about?

During my (Eddy's) college years, I knew that even as a layperson, I was called to minister. But ministry, as I understood it, involved only meeting spiritual needs.

While I was growing up, my Christianity had consisted mainly of observing a list of dos and don'ts. Do go to church faithfully. Don't steal or lie. Do read your Bible and pray every day. Don't smoke or drink. Do pay your tithe. Don't go to dances or movies. Do obey your parents. Don't fight with your brother or sister. If I could just do all the dos and not do all the don'ts, I believed, then I would be a "good Christian."

One afternoon, probably about my sophomore year in high school, I lay on my bed mentally running through my checklist. I felt reassured by my high score. I was doing all the dos and avoiding all the don'ts—except for one. (The one about my brother and sister just might have slipped my mind that day.) The one thing I knew I wasn't doing, that I knew I had to be doing to be a good Christian, was witnessing.

The thought of trying to witness terrified me, probably mostly because I was so shy. But I was convinced I had to witness to be a good Christian, and the thought of going to hell terrified me even more—so I resolved to begin witnessing.

The next year at school I organized a Bible club. Over the next two years the club conducted on-campus Bible studies, handed out evangelistic tracts, placed Bibles in every classroom, and sponsored morning devotions over the intercom. I confidently checked off the last item on my "good Christian" checklist.

Once I went off to college, my witnessing usually took the form of spending Sunday afternoons in a park with several other Nazarene college students approaching strangers with *The Four Spiritual Laws*, a booklet that explained how to become a Christian. A half dozen or so of the people I talked to prayed the sinner's prayer. One even came to church afterward for a few months.

But in time we grew uneasy with our cold-turkey approach to witnessing. One reason was that we saw little evidence that it was leading to changed lives. But part of my discomfort, I believe, stemmed from my own changing relationship with God. Nurtured by my pastor's sermons, I was seeing God less as a critical Judge—making a list and checking it twice—and more as a loving Father. I was beginning to realize that God wasn't just concerned about my getting to heaven; He also cared about my joys and pains, my hopes and fears. He was willing to guide me when I was confused, provide for me when I was in need, strengthen me when I was weak, comfort me when I grieved. God didn't just care about my soul; He cared about me as a whole person.

The more I experienced God's love, the more clear it became that I was not treating my witnessing prospects the way God treated me. I was treating them as objects, as trophies to be won, not as hurting people who needed to be loved.

Somehow early on I had gotten the idea that ministry

involved only—or at least primarily—meeting spiritual needs. Evangelizing, preaching, teaching the Bible, praying, spiritual counseling, leading worship—this was ministry. But feeding the hungry? Visiting the sick? Welcoming strangers? If you would have asked me, I probably would have put such activities into the same category as joining the Boy Scouts—perhaps nice to do, but hardly anything God expected. I had not yet learned to see the dirty feet in my world.

But as love replaced law as my motivation for ministry, I started seeing other people through new eyes. I became less concerned with persuading others to do the right thing and more concerned with meeting their needs. With this change in motivation it also became obvious to me that ministry had to be concerned not just with spiritual needs but with the needs of the total person. Love, I was beginning to see, cannot limit itself to caring about only one kind of need.

This growing awareness that God's love compels us to respond to the needs of the whole person would eventually lead our family to join two others in moving to a low-income inner-city neighborhood to share the gospel with our new neighbors through ministries that responded to both spiritual and social needs. We held backyard Bible schools, helped run a shelter for homeless families, taught English as a second language, and started a prayer and Bible study group. After a couple of years, our family started taking homeless families into our own home for periods ranging from two weeks to several months while we tried to help them stabilize their lives. Ten years later, some of the people who then lived with us still write or call us to ask for prayer and spiritual counsel.

How did Jesus love?

Jesus ministered to every conceivable kind of need—

He forgave sins, healed the sick, taught His disciples, and championed the oppressed. In a society that saw women as vastly inferior, He treated women and men with equal respect. In a synagogue while surrounded by racist Jews, He proclaimed God's equal love for Gentiles, even though He must have known His audience would try to kill Him (Luke 4:25-29). Jesus spent so much time with people others looked down on that His enemies branded Him the "friend of tax collectors and 'sinners'" (Matt. 11:19).

Jesus calls us to respond to people's needs in the same way He did. "I was hungry and you gave me something to eat," He said, "I was thirsty and you gave me something to drink, I was a stranger and you invited me in, I needed clothes and you clothed me, I was sick and you looked after me, I was in prison and you came to visit me. . . . whatever you did for one of the least of these brothers of mine, you did for me" (Matt. 25:35-36, 40). Especially amazing to those of us who grew up seeing such things as optional are Jesus' words that those who do such things will receive eternal life and those who do not will receive eternal punishment (v. 46).

God calls us to minister to both spiritual and social needs. To respond to one and not to the other is to fail to love as God loves. It is to fail to live out the gospel.

Behold, how they love

In the first century, non-Christians would remark of Christians, "Behold, how they love one another." Today when Christians respond with love to people in need, the world still takes notice.

On Sunday, December 29, 1991, while on his way to church, Steve Lamb was involved in a car accident that caused a serious head injury. He was rushed to Mercy Hospital in Oklahoma City, where he lay in a coma. From the hospital, Steve's wife, Cyndi, called the church where the morning service was in progress.

"People from our church came to the hospital and stayed with me all day long," Cyndi says. As people left to go home that night, Cyndi faced the prospect of spending the night alone as she waited for updates on Steve's condition. About ten o'clock, her friend Debbie showed up with blankets and pillows and announced, "I'm here to camp out with you."

Cyndi remembers, "From that day until Steve was transferred to a Dallas hospital in April, every weekday someone from the church came to the hospital to be with me. Twice a week, people from the church would bring us meals, usually enough food to make four meals. Once a week someone would come by to do my grocery shopping and run errands for me. Since we lived in Edmond and the church is in Bethany, this wasn't convenient for any of them. They all lived 30 minutes away."

This was all coordinated through sign-up sheets at the church, but Cyndi was impressed that none of it was initiated by church staff. It was all done by laypeople.

The people of the church have given not only their time but also their prayers. Within a few weeks of the accident, one woman in the church started hosting a prayer meeting for Steve and the family every Tuesday in her home. A year later the group is still meeting weekly to pray.

During those first weeks after the accident, Cyndi remembers thinking, This is wonderful, but will anyone be here in a month? The weeks turned into months and, as this is being written, Steve has been hospitalized more than a year. Though his recovery has been slow, the caring support of Christian friends has been constant.

The Lambs had excellent medical insurance but no disability insurance, leaving the family with no income. Cyndi's friends didn't want her to have to go to work right away. They felt she needed to be free to take care of her

sons, Jeremy and Tate, aged 11 and 6, and spend time regularly with Steve at the hospital. Besides that, a baby was on
the way, and they wanted her to be able to be at home with
the baby.

"God has met our financial needs in two ways,"
Cyndi explains. "First, people began giving us services at
no charge—dental and medical care, haircuts, oil changes,
car repairs. One man in our church gave me a credit card
and told me to charge all my gasoline to that card. For a
year now, I haven't paid a cent for gasoline. Another
church member who has a landscaping business added me
to his route but didn't charge me. He did all kinds of
things for our lawn that we'd never done before. We had
the best-looking lawn in Edmond.

"About February a couple of men set up a fund for our
family at the church and sent out a letter asking people to
give to it. Now I just take my bills to the church, and the
church pays them out of that fund. There's always been
more than enough to meet our needs. I haven't had to
spend one moment worrying about finances.

"Of all that people have done," says Cyndi, "most
meaningful to me as a mother is what people have done
for my children. From the beginning, several families have
gone out of their way to include my boys in what they are
doing. For example, this last Christmas vacation, the first
anniversary of the accident, was an especially difficult time
for us. Though it had been a full year after the accident,
people were still going out of their way to include my
boys. A man from the church took Jeremy and Tate bowl-
ing with his boys. The next day another family took them
horseback riding with their girls. The next day it was an
invitation to a science museum, and the next day an invitation to watch a ball game on big-screen TV. They've been
taken to rodeos, on camp-outs and fishing trips, and to col-

lege football games. It doesn't make up for not having Steve, but it does a lot for them."

Being dependent on the generosity of others can be hard for anyone. Cyndi remembers, "When this happened, I felt like God said to me, 'You're not going to make it unless you can let others help you.' I realized I could no longer keep tabs, so I've been able to relax and freely accept God's lavish provision."

The church's outpouring of love to the Lambs is an excellent example of whole-person ministry—ministering to spiritual, financial, practical, and emotional needs—but the Lambs aren't the only ones who have been ministered to in the process.

Cindy Penick is a secretary whose boss, Mark, was one of those coordinating the help for the Lambs. Before Steve's accident, Mark had been inviting her to church for a year, but she had never come. In the days after the accident, as many as 10 people a day would call Mark at the office to check on Steve's condition or offer help. People would come by the office, and Cindy would be amazed at how much they cared.

"Mark told me how people were giving out of their pockets to help the Lambs, but I didn't believe it," Cindy says. "There was no way people could give like that without wanting to get something out of it for themselves."

So impressed was Cindy that the next time Mark invited her to church, she went, but she was still skeptical. She did not believe what she was seeing could be for real. "But," says Cindy, "the first Sunday people were so welcoming and loving, I went back. In the coming weeks, the more I heard what people were doing for the Lambs, the more overwhelmed I was."

Cindy and her children have been going to church ever since. In fact, she has joined the church and found her own ministry working in the church nursery. Most important of all, though, is that for the first time in her life, God is real and personal to her.

"God had always been distant to me," she said. "I didn't know I could talk to Him. Now He's a personal friend. And the change I've seen in my family this last year has been truly amazing. I feel like I've found a home."

Win Arn, a leader in the church growth movement, writes, "Ministry in its purest and simplest form is love. . . . Ministry is, in fact, doing love!"[1] When we respond to hurting people with loving, whole-person ministry, the world cannot help but notice, and people will be drawn to Christ.

A liberating call

Does it sound like good news to hear that God calls us to minister not just to spiritual needs but to all kinds of needs? Or does it sound as if God is expecting you to do so much you can't possibly do it all? It could sound that way. But the good news is that while God does call us to respond to every kind of need, He doesn't expect any of us to do it alone.

While no one person can effectively reach out to every kind of need, all of us working together can! God has placed within the Body of Christ all the spiritual gifts needed to minister to the many needs both within the Body and in the world around us.

Far from being burdensome, the call to whole-person ministry can be liberating to someone whose understanding of ministry has been limited to meeting spiritual needs. Because they are not gifted in evangelism, Bible teaching, spiritual counseling, or any of the other areas that focus primarily on spiritual needs, some deeply committed Christians have spent years feeling guilty and frustrated about their personal ministries.

Often the reason for their frustration is simple: God has given them abilities that minister primarily to other kinds of needs. If your spiritual gift is serving, you may find joy in repairing cars or buildings, in helping friends move, in cleaning, in running errands for a friend. If it is showing mercy, you may be best at taking meals to shut-ins, caring for the sick or disabled, or visiting nursing home residents. If encouragement is your gift, you may be good at supporting someone through a crisis or motivating others to do what is right even when it is difficult. Maybe your gift is giving to others' needs. You may not be very good at any of these things, yet be gifted at coordinating the efforts of those who are.

Think of what a crucial role each of these spiritual gifts played in ministering to the Lambs. No one person could have met such a wide range of needs, but by working together, the Body of Christ met all the needs.

If you have had trouble finding your ministry, could it be because your definition of ministry has been too narrow? Can you think of one way God uses you to meet another person's need? Any kind of need? If you can, you have just named one way you minister.

A Nazarene rediscovers his roots

If any church has reason to champion whole-person ministry, the Church of the Nazarene does. David Best's story suggests why.

David was a third-generation Nazarene. His grandmother had been a charter member of the Whittier, Calif., church, and his father was a Nazarene pastor. Yet it was not at all clear to David whether there was a place for him in the Church of the Nazarene.

As a boy, David had a vision of ministry that had been shaped by his Grandfather Highley, an evangelist who took with him Black song evangelist Albert Tindley wherever he held revivals, sometimes to places where Blacks had never before been welcomed. He had heard his mom tell of going to Jamaica for several months to do volunteer work with Black evangelical leader Clarence Jacobs. Back in the U.S. when a woman at church had asked his mom, "Is he your chauffeur?" she had answered, "No, he's my brother." Clarence Jacobs would later become pastor of the Brooklyn Miller Memorial Church of the Nazarene.

David had heard how his mom and grandfather had gone out into the orange orchards to sing and share the gospel with migrant workers and then asked, "Now, is there anything we can do for you?" They said they needed help cashing checks, buying work clothes and other personal items, and getting dress patterns for their wives, sisters, and mothers back home.

"It was a thrill," David's mother remembered, "to see their smiles when we returned with the results of our shopping trip." Before David was born, his mother and grandfather had been combining evangelism and compassionate ministries.

When he was eight or nine, David and his brother had gone with their grandfather to help him remodel church buildings for Black congregations in Watts, south central Los Angeles. Seven years later, when Watts burned for the first time, David felt it as a personal loss. He knew something was terribly wrong.

David went on to Pasadena College, but he wrestled with big questions about his faith. Was Christianity the real thing? Was Jesus God's only Son? In time he was able to confidently answer yes to those questions, but he had more trouble with what he calls "this church thing."

"My church taught me that if I had a personal relationship with God, I was a Christian," he said. "And if I could help others have a personal relationship with God, I was doing what I was supposed to do.

"All that was OK, but it wasn't enough. It seemed to me there was something wrong with a faith that had little impact on my life outside the area of my private piety. Hell was breaking out all around—race riots, political assassinations, the Vietnam War—and my church seemed to have no positive response to it."

Disillusioned with a church that seemed unable to relate the gospel to the deep hurts and conflicts that were tearing society apart, he even considered changing denominations. Should he become an Episcopalian? Or perhaps a Mennonite?

During college he had heard lectures about Phineas Bresee, founder of the Church of the Nazarene, and John Wesley, the founder of the movement from which the denomination sprang; but it was not until a few years after graduation that David began to actually read them for himself.

"I was impressed with Bresee's concern for the poor and the dispossessed," he said. "He had a social understanding of the gospel. In fact, he opposed the alcohol industry so vigorously that they hanged him in effigy. I saw how Wesley was driven to reach those who weren't being reached and was willing to try almost anything to accomplish that. He hated field preaching. He much preferred to preach from behind the 'consecrated desk,' but he was willing to do whatever worked, and so he spent much of his life preaching in the fields."

Seeing how Bresee combined personal spirituality with social witness and how Wesley innovated to reach out to those outside the church was liberating for David. "I realized I didn't have to become an Episcopalian or Mennonite; I could be a Nazarene."

Today David is pastor of the Lamb's Manhattan Church of the Nazarene, which meets just off Times Square in New York City. This congregation's ministries range from an off-Broadway theater to a Cocaine Anonymous group to a health clinic for Manhattan's homeless people. In these and all their other outreaches, David believes the church is proclaiming God's good news.

Moustapha's first contact with the Lamb's Church was when he came into the clinic asking for cough medicine. The doctor gave him the medicine, then asked, "Do you need anything else?"

"Yeh, I'm on drugs," he answered.

"Do you want to get off?"

"Of course, I want off. But who can get off drugs?" Moustapha wanted to know.

The doctor's next question took the patient completely by surprise. "Do you know Christ?"

"What does Christ have to do with this?" Moustapha wanted to know. The idea that Christianity could help him with his drug problem was totally foreign to him.

Moustapha had been born and raised in a Muslim family in Senegal, West Africa. His father, who had eight wives, was the head of his tribal village. Of his 50 or 60 children, Moustapha had been one of his favorites, and as a child Moustapha had studied the Koran so that he could succeed his father as the village's spiritual leader.

Later his brother had loaned him money so that he could come to the United States to study business and return to Senegal to work in his business with him. But while in school, Moustapha had started using and pushing drugs, used up his brother's money, and found himself living on the streets. By the time he came into the Lamb's clinic, he had been living on the streets of New York for several years.

But although the idea of Christ being able to help him with his drug addiction was totally new to him, a few weeks after the doctor's invitation, Moustapha came to church for the first time. Two to three months later, he accepted Christ.

He immediately got involved in the church's discipleship program. The church offered him housing on the sixth floor of The Lamb's Center in exchange for work in the counseling center. On Pentecost Sunday, 1991, Moustapha was baptized. He is now working full-time for the church —part-time with social services and part-time with counseling services.

For Moustapha, Christianity is good news.

David Best's definition of ministry is simple. "Ministry is loving people like Jesus would. It is serving people in God's name so that He gets the glory."

The Lamb's Manhattan Church is only one example of how the Church of the Nazarene is rediscovering its roots as a movement among the poor. More and more, the denomination is returning to the inner cities. More churches are being planted among ethnic minorities.

Many churches and districts have formed Compassionate Ministry committees to respond to people in need. Throughout the world, Compassionate Ministry centers are operating as rescue missions, drug treatment centers, shelters for the homeless, employment training centers, health clinics, counseling centers, and more. Never before have so many Nazarenes been so involved in ministry to the whole person.

God calls each of us to different kinds of ministry, but He calls all of us to wash dirty feet. Who are the hurting people whose lives you can touch with God's love? What needs do you see that are going unmet because not enough people care? Where in your world are the dirty feet?

Will you say yes to God's call to be a foot washer?

A lone man, a pastor, stands in a church sanctuary, surrounded by empty seats. "The church is most the church," he says into the camera, "when the sanctuary is empty."[1] *James Garlow, pastor of Metroplex Chapel in Dallas-Fort Worth, is tackling yet another myth—that most of the church's ministry takes place when the church is gathered.*

3

THE EMPTY SANCTUARY

One night in July 1987, Jim Couchenour got a phone call that would change the outward course of his life.

A member of the Columbiana, Ohio, Church of the Nazarene, Jim had invested himself wholeheartedly in the work of the church for many years. He was on the church board, chairman of the finance committee, head of the development committee, and a member of the choir. On the district he was serving with the Advisory Board and on the Finance Committee. He was a trustee of Mount Vernon Nazarene College. He served with the Association of Nazarene Building Professionals, on the General Board, and on various commissions and assignments for the general church. Here, in his own words, is Jim's story of how that evening phone call sparked a radical change in his approach to ministry.

Sam,* a close friend of mine who had a drinking problem, had gotten upset at home that evening and stormed out of the house. His wife, Diane,* was afraid he was headed for the tavern. She called to ask if I would please go look for him. Of course I told her I would.

I put on my jeans and went down to the town's only tavern. Not sure I wanted anyone to see me going in, I went around to the back. I walked up to a woman sitting by the back door and said, "I'm looking for a fellow named Sam."

*Names have been changed.

"He's not here," she said. "Furthermore, he's not going to be here. He owes me $123 for a bar bill, and the police know he's not to be admitted back in here again."

I thanked her and left.

I didn't find Sam that night, but as I prayed that evening and the next morning, God laid a strange request on me. I was to go back down to the tavern and offer to pay Sam's bar bill.

Now I was raised in a Nazarene parsonage. I've been in the church all my life, and I'd never been in a tavern before. That would be the first bar bill I'd ever paid.

I went back that night and asked for Nellie. I'd heard she operated the tavern. Someone pointed to a woman sitting on a barstool, playing cards with the bartender. It was the same woman I'd met the night before.

I sat down on the stool next to her and introduced myself.

"I remember you from last night," she said.

"Nellie," I said, "I'm here partly because I'm concerned about my friend Sam, but I also know you have a business to run. I have some cash here; I'd like to pay something on Sam's bar bill." I gave her the $90.00 I had in my pocket, and she thanked me.

I sat for 20 minutes that night talking to Nellie Watson. I found out that this 65-year-old lady, way back in her early childhood, had gone to Sunday School. She'd even taught Sunday School once and had a vague belief in prayer.

I left that night, not expecting to ever go back again. But God had other ideas. The next morning as I prayed, God laid on my heart a ridiculous request— that I go back down to Nellie's and ask her if she would let a gospel singing group put on a concert in the tavern some Saturday night.

That night I was back in the tavern. "Nellie," I said, "I think you really care about the people who come in here, and I do too, but I don't know them. I don't think they'd ever come to church, but how would you feel about us bringing a religious singing group down here and putting on a concert?"

She sat there for a moment, then said, "That's a great idea."

A week from that following Saturday night, five people from our local church went down to Young's Tavern and for two hours sang to that tavern crowd. It was one of the most fascinating evenings of my life. Nellie would get my attention and point to someone. I'd go over and sit on the barstool alongside the person, and within 90 seconds he or she would be sharing important life concerns. We'd talk a little bit, then Nellie would get my attention and point to someone else. I'd go to the next person, and the same thing would happen. Over and over again that night, we dispensed Phil. 4:4, 6-7: "Rejoice in the Lord always. . . . Do not be anxious about anything, but in everything, by prayer and petition, with thanksgiving, present your requests to God. And the peace of God, which transcends all understanding, will guard your hearts and your minds in Christ Jesus."

The next Wednesday I went back. As I walked through the back door, Nellie said, "Oh, boy, am I glad to see you. Here's a fellow I want you to talk to. John, get over here. This is the guy I was telling you about." Then she explained, "John here is trying to quit drinking, but he needs to know where to go to AA meetings, and I figured you could help him." Well, I knew nothing about Alcoholics Anonymous meetings; but I did talk to John, and we were later able to direct him to an AA group.

Every Wednesday for the next six months, rather than going to church for prayer meeting, I went back to the tavern. Every single Wednesday night, someone was either waiting for me or someone came in while I was there, wanting help for a problem. I kind of became the chaplain of Young's Tavern, and other

Christians from my church got involved in the ministry as well.

Along about September one of the fellows at the tavern said, "I wish we had more time to talk." So we started going back to the tavern after church on Sunday nights to talk with whoever wanted to talk about spiritual things. I have never found it so easy to share about God and His love.

At Christmastime one of the men of the church provided a full-course dinner free of charge to the tavern people. That night we held another Christian concert.

In January 1988, Nellie closed the tavern both for financial reasons and because of a growing awareness that she shouldn't be involved in this sort of thing. When the tavern closed, we kept the Wednesday and Sunday night sessions going in homes. One cold February evening in a small-group meeting, Nellie Watson gave her heart to Jesus Christ.

The lady who had operated the bar before Nellie took it over was a friend of Nellie's. Nellie invited her to church and she came. She recommitted her life to God and is now a member of the Nazarene church in Columbiana. The same thing began happening in other people's lives.

In July God told me to resign from the church board. I had no idea why God was telling me to do that after all these years. But God knew. He knew that in the fall we would find the building He had in mind for a ministry that would open in December.[2]

Today what started as a tavern ministry has grown into a multifaceted outreach called The Way Station. In a building near the former tavern, Jim and other volunteers installed pool tables, a foosball table, a pinball machine, and other games. The Way Station is open seven nights a week from 7 P.M. until 1 A.M. In addition to the nightly drop-in fellowship, the center sponsors support groups for drug addicts, survivors of sexual abuse, adults raised in dysfunctional homes, and people with eating disorders. There are

Bible studies, prayer meetings, English-as-a-second-language classes, programs for children and retired persons, and concerts. Emergency transportation, food, clothing, and a crisis referral service are always available. The Way Station is now staffed by more than 30 volunteers and a full-time youth minister.

Jim says:

God introduced us to the world of dilated eyes of marijuana, the flaring nostrils of cocaine, financial needs, and other burdens most of us cannot comprehend. He showed me that this world is going to hell without us laypeople doing what He wants us to do. I've lived in Columbiana 28 years. All these needs, all these problems, all this hopelessness was there all the time that I was living with my nice family, my nice church people, my nice committee people. Right in my hometown there was a mission field as cross-cultural as any mission field in the world.[3]

Jim would eventually resign from all but one of the church boards and commissions he had served on before The Way Station started, but his story does not mean that everyone who holds a position in the church should resign it and start a ministry in the community. It does, though, show the danger the church faces of becoming ingrown and being content with maintaining its traditional ministries while all around it hurting people are crying out for help. And it demonstrates that like Jim and the others involved in The Way Station, we all need to let the Holy Spirit create within us a sensitivity to people's needs— wherever they are.

Why does the church gather?

In many congregations the ministries of the church scattered have received less attention than the ministries of the church gathered. "Perhaps the greatest threat [to] the Christian Church today," writes James Garlow, "is the threat of 'ingrownness,' so focusing on itself and its own needs that it fails to remember the purpose for which it was called into existence."[4] Some churches have in fact become ingrown. They have forgotten that one critical reason for coming together is to be equipped for ministry so that each member can then be sent out to minister every day of the week.

In some ways the church is like a sales team. When the sales team meets, its members may celebrate recent accomplishments. Sales managers may try to inspire and motivate the team, to give them a vision of what is possible. Group members may encourage one another or empathize with each other's difficulties. This all helps to build a sense of community—group members feel they are not alone, but part of a team. Some meetings include training to equip each salesperson to do a more effective job.

Now what would you think of that sales team if, upon leaving the meeting, the members made little or no effort to sell? Would you suspect they missed the point of the meeting?

We in the church are not a sales team but a ministry team, yet we gather for many of these same reasons—to celebrate, to expand our vision, to be inspired to fulfill our mission, to give and receive encouragement, and to be equipped for ministry. If, then, at the end of our gathering we go out into the world but make little attempt to minister, what does that suggest? Could it be that we missed the point of why we came together?

I (Eddy) recently visited an adult Sunday School class and came away convinced that the teacher and class officers knew exactly why the class came together every Sunday. To begin with, they came together for fellowship, to give and receive friendship and encouragement. Their class calendar showed several upcoming fellowship events outside the Sunday morning time slot. Many had been together in the class for years and had formed deep friendships. The class was fulfilling many of the New Testament commands to minister to one another.

But this class came together for more than fellowship. If you had been with me that morning, you would have heard one class member describe how persons often give gifts to poor children at Christmas but sometimes overlook the fact that poor children may have nothing to give their parents. For years this class had supported a local shelter for homeless families with their money, many hours of volunteer work, and their love. This Christmas, class members were being invited to buy gifts that children at the shelter could in turn give their parents.

You would have heard another class member make an announcement about the visitation schedule for a husband and wife who were serving prison sentences for actions they had taken before becoming Christians. So many people from the church—about half of them from this one class—were wanting to visit this couple that the prison wouldn't let any more on the visitation list. But, the class member explained, it was possible to rotate people on and off the list. A prayer request for the husband was shared, and class members were reminded to send the wife cards on her birthday.

You would have listened to a Sunday School lesson about ministering to family members, one that was not merely theoretical but called for specific practical application.

When I left that class, I knew I had been in the presence of a teacher who understood that her job was not simply to teach a Sunday School lesson but to equip her class members to wash dirty feet, to minister seven days a week to people in need wherever they were—within the church, within their families, in their communities, or in the world beyond their communities.

Ministry within the church

Though most ministry takes place when the church is scattered, not gathered, our ministry is to begin within the Christian family. Paul wrote, "Whenever we have an opportunity, let us work for the good of all, and *especially for those of the family of faith*" (Gal. 6:10, NRSV, emphasis added).

We all are ministered to by others in the family of faith. Most of us who grew up in the church can look back on Sunday School teachers whose love and caring made a lasting difference in our lives. We appreciate the pianist, organist, and choir members who help us worship each Sunday. We depend on janitors and gardeners to make the church building and grounds look loved and welcoming. Ushering and greeting, far from being simple chores, can be powerful ministries when done by those who see them that way.

Bill Harris' days as a greeter began one Sunday morning more than 35 years ago. When he noticed that someone needed help finding a chair in his crowded Sunday School class, he jumped up and showed the person a seat. He has been a greeter ever since. For the past 13 years he has been greeting people at the curbside as they arrive for church.

"I've always wanted to make people feel comfortable and at home," Bill says. "If I notice someone standing alone in a crowd, I'll often go up and talk to him." Bill has the important ministry of making people feel welcome.

When the church gathers, we depend on the ministries of all these people and more. But what if your gifts don't fit any of these particular roles? Do you have a ministry within the Body of Christ?

Indeed you do. We all do. We all can minister within the body, whatever our gifts. This is because most ministry in the body does not involve carrying out the responsibilities of a position. It comes through simple acts of caring, one person to another.

The "one another" commands of the New Testament —"Be devoted to one another," "Accept one another," "Serve one another," "Bear one another's burdens," "Encourage one another," "Love one another" (Rom. 12:10; 15:7; Gal. 5:13; 6:2, NRSV; Heb. 10:25, etc.; John 13:34-35, etc.), and many more—all describe how we are to relate to fellow believers. I can minister with a hug on Sunday morning; an encouraging phone call during the week; saying, "I'll pray for you," then doing it; baby-sitting so that parents can have a night out; putting an anonymous gift in the mail to help with a medical bill. The first Christian church described in Acts did such a good job of caring for each other's material needs that it was said of them, "There were no needy persons among them" (4:34). Can that be said of your church?

Ministering to each other's personal needs, all kinds of needs, as an expression of the love God gives us for one another is at the very heart of authentic church life. One bumper sticker reads, "Practice random acts of kindness and senseless acts of beauty." It is these daily acts of love that bind us together and show the world that we are Jesus' followers.

Ministry to your family

Not all of us have spouses or children, but those who do not usually have other family nearby or family-like relationships. For people who are serious about ministry, it is sometimes tempting to get caught up in ministry within the church, in the community, or across the ocean and shortchange our ministry to those who sit across our kitchen table.

I (Eddy) loved my work as director of an inner-city ministry organization. Almost every morning I woke up excited about going to the office, eager to plunge into the work of planning, counseling, and teaching.

Though my wife tried to tell me, it was not until I had left that job that I realized how much I had neglected my own family during those years. I had not been the kind of husband or father my family needed. I realized I had to find a way to make ministry to my family priority over my work.

Though I had been thinking of returning to inner-city ministry, I concluded that I needed a job that demanded less of my time and energy, at least while our children were young.

I got a job as a secretary. To go from being the director of a ministry organization to being a secretary is not the kind of career move the world applauds—or even understands—but it was a decision God honored.

Within a few months I was able to cut my secretarial job back to four days a week to spend one day a week on my writing. A year later my free-lance writing business had grown to the point that I could resign my secretarial job and write full-time.

Today I enjoy writing just as much as I enjoyed inner-city ministry, and it seldom takes more than 40 hours a week. Best of all, because I work at home I get to help teach home school and can be there for my family whenever I am needed.

It costs to make ministry to family a top priority, sometimes in career advancement, sometimes in income, sometimes both. But the rewards are beyond anything money can buy.

Ministry to your community

Shortly after Roy Eagan sold his plumbing business to retire, he went to the administrator of the Children's Convalescent Center in Bethany, Okla., a center for the long-term care of seriously handicapped children, and told him, "I'm here to work." While doing plumbing work for the center earlier, Roy had noticed some maintenance needs going unmet. Now that he had time, he wanted to volunteer.

When Roy offered his help, the administrator told his secretary, "Lock the door and get a time card!" And that is how Roy became the new maintenance person—part paid, part volunteer—at the convalescent center.

But Roy became much more than a maintenance person. Working day after day among handicapped children separated from their families, Roy became the resident "papa" for many of the children.

On Roy's 75th birthday, the children at the convalescent center threw him a party. One four-year-old girl, on behalf of all the children, gave Roy a shirt. On the front it says, "Super Papa," and on the back, "He works for hugs."

Local organizations such as food pantries, shelters for the homeless, and crisis pregnancy centers are great places to find "dirty feet." Many churches operate ministries of community outreach such as Meals on Wheels, Mothers' Day Out, or after-school programs for latchkey children.

Some Christians minister by serving on school boards or in local government. Others participate in civic organizations and professional societies. Sometimes we may view such involvements as taking time away from ministry, because they are not church-related. While God will not lead every Christian to join such organizations, participation can provide opportunities to build relationships with others in our communities and minister to their needs.

Ministry to the world

Sometimes what starts out as a local ministry grows to have a broader impact. Gary and Janalee Hoffman, members of First Church of the Nazarene in Las Vegas, Nev., sensed God's call to begin visiting inmates at a medium-security prison in Jean, Nev. That ministry expanded after Henry, one of Gary's former employees, was convicted of murder and sentenced to Nevada's death row. Before Henry started serving his sentence, he committed his life to the Lord. Shortly after arriving on death row, he started asking Gary and Jan for Christian literature he could give to his fellow prisoners in Carson City. Soon Gary and Jan found themselves corresponding with most of the 36 men on Nevada's death row.

The Hoffmans were surprised to discover 12 believers on death row but dismayed to learn that because of the work load, prison chaplains rarely visited these Christian brothers. The men were physically separated from each other and isolated from any personal ministry. Janalee began praying for a way to help draw these men together so that they could encourage one another. The plan the Lord gave was for a Christian newsletter written for and by death row convicts. The ministry of *The Rising Son* newsletter, started as an attempt to bring together the men on Nevada's death row, has expanded rapidly. It now reaches 6,000 prisoners in 152 penitentiaries in all 50 states of the United States and in 32 other countries.

The Heart to Heart project is another ministry that started out small, then mushroomed. It began as a small effort, spearheaded by a group of Nazarene laypeople through a local civic club, to gather medicines and medical supplies for the people of the former Soviet Union. To the great surprise of the organizers, the project gained the support of thousands of people throughout the American Midwest, as well as the interest of the media. Grocery stores sponsored drives to collect donated over-the-counter medicines, and pharmaceutical companies pitched in. Over 90 tons of medicines and supplies were donated, with a value of over $5 million. The U.S. Air Force provided its largest plane, the C-5 Galaxy, to airlift the donations to Moscow, where they were distributed to hospitals and clinics on behalf of the Church of the Nazarene, the Union of Evangelical Christians, and the Moscow Rotary Club.

Of course, most of us will not start prison ministries or organize airlifts, but we can all support the church's mission of world evangelization through prayer, encouragement, and financial support. In recent years thousands of Nazarene laypeople have become actively involved in ministering to those in other parts of the world through programs like Work and Witness, short-term volunteer assignments, Nazarenes In Volunteer Service (NIVS), and others, both through our denomination as well as through other mission and parachurch organizations.

Ministry to the world, however, is not limited to the traditional overseas mission fields. In most cases, we no longer have to travel long distances to minister cross-culturally. The world has been brought to our doorstep. People from various cultures, ethnic groups, and nationalities now live in most of our cities and on most of our university campuses. Never before have we had so many opportunities to minister to the peoples of the world right in our own backyard.

Each of us is surrounded by scores of opportunities to minister—within our churches, to our families, to our communities, and to the world. None of us can say yes to every need. But we can all say yes to those to which God calls us.

Some are called to minister to the church gathered. But most of the church's ministry is to take place when the sanctuary is empty, when the church is scattered.

One church regularly reminded its members of this by placing above the sanctuary exit a sign that said, "Servants' Entrance." This coming Sunday as you leave your church's sanctuary, remember: You're not leaving the church behind; you're taking the church to the world. You, as a member of the Body of Christ, are being sent out to proclaim God's good news by word and deed to a world that desperately needs God's love.

＊＊

Many laypeople feel that because of their work they have fewer opportunities to minister than do ministry professionals. In fact, most laypeople have an access to people outside the church that most ministry professionals will never have.
Being a layperson, far from limiting your ministry opportunities, actually puts you on the front lines.

＊＊

4

THE MYTH OF SECULAR WORK

Jan Lundy runs a ministry organization, but you won't find it listed in the Yellow Pages under that heading. You'll have to look under "Laboratories." Her business, Precision Histology, is a medical laboratory in Oklahoma City where microscope slides of tissues are prepared from which doctors diagnose patients' illnesses.

Precision Histology has been going for 10 years now, and, as the world measures success, it hasn't made much of a splash. For the first few years Jan had to reinvest all her earnings into the company to buy equipment, and today she earns only a modest wage. But that's OK with Jan, because Precision Histology is succeeding at what it was created to do.

"From the beginning our main purpose has been to help people," Jan explains. This happens in various ways. Jan hired lab technicians with little or no technical skill and gave them on-the-job training. Often these were mothers from low-income families who lacked the resources to pay for formal training. One technician she hired was already trained but was recovering from drug addiction and not physically able to go back to work in the hospital.

Jan also made it possible for employees to keep their children with them at work by providing a play area at the lab and, when necessary, hiring a child care worker at no cost to the mothers.

Karen, one of Jan's first trainees, has recently returned to work for Jan full-time after gaining hospital experience. "Jan gave me a job when I had no job and no training to get a job," she says. "Christy was just six weeks old then, and because Jan made it possible for me to keep Christy with me at work, I was able to nurse her."

Jan relates to her employees not just as individuals but as families, including spouses and children in company social events. And, of course, in all these relationships she tries to show God's love and share her faith in appropriate ways.

As part of its ministry, the lab has prepared slides at no charge for three local nonprofit clinics serving low-income patients.

But most basic of all, the lab ministers through the services it is paid to provide. As the name she chose for her company implies, Jan insists upon work of the highest quality, both from herself and her employees. "I treat each slide as though it is for a member of my own family," Jan says. "After all, each one is for *somebody's* mother, brother, or sister."

Once when a lab employee delivered slides to a client, the doctor noticed a problem with one of them. He told the employee, "I know Jan will take care of this, because she's very religious." That doctor recognized that the conscientiousness he had come to expect from Precision Histology was a direct expression of Jan's faith.

"Caring whether people have a good diagnosis is very important to me," says Jan. "Doctors need to be able to interpret slides easily and accurately. If my slides enable them to do that, I am ministering to the patients whether they know it or not." Most of the people to whom Jan and her coworkers minister, then, are people they never meet, but that doesn't make their ministry any less real or important.

Secular or sacred?

God does not view work the way our culture does. Our culture identifies a few vocations—those involving "professional ministry"—as sacred. Other vocations—such as being an accountant, sanitation worker, homemaker, or mechanic—it labels secular. These jobs, according to the conventional wisdom, are not concerned with religion.

But God is not willing for us to divide life into the religious and nonreligious, the secular and the holy. He calls us to so live that our entire lives are sacred. Paul writes, "So whether you eat or drink or whatever you do, do it all for the glory of God" (1 Cor. 10:31). God calls us to do everything we do, from eating breakfast in the morning to working during the day to playing with our kids in the evening, with the purpose of bringing glory to God—causing others to think more highly of Him. For the Christian, every aspect of life, every moment of every day, is to be holy.

Ministering *through* our work means more than simply ministering *while at* work. Many Christians look for appropriate opportunities to talk about their faith with coworkers, clients, or customers. This is important, but ministering through our work goes beyond this. Some minister by modeling such Christian virtues as honesty, respect, and diligence in workplaces where lying, put-downs, and loafing are the norm. Such integrity can be a powerful witness. But ministering through our work goes still further.

Ministering through our work means ministering to people's needs by the very work we do. Is this possible? Is it possible to minister by the act of baking bread? By the act of typing a letter? By the act of changing a diaper or washing dishes? Is it possible to minister by the act of driving a truck or building a house?

If we understand that ministry is not restricted to

meeting spiritual needs but includes responding in Christian love to any kind of need, the answer is *yes*. You may have been ministering through your work for many years, even if you haven't known to call it that.

Does this mean that all workers minister through their work? No, it doesn't. Whether your work is also ministry depends on the kind of work you do and the spirit in which you do it.

Test No. 1: Does your work meet needs?

In the New Testament, the primary word for ministry is *diakonia*, which means service. If you compare different versions of the New Testament, you'll find that the various forms of *diakonia* are often translated "service" and "serve" in one version and "ministry" and "minister" in another, or even in different ways within the same version. To minister, then, is to serve. It is to meet another's need.

When Jan Lundy or one of her employees prepares a slide, they are meeting a need. They are helping diagnose a patient's illness so that the doctor can prescribe appropriate treatment.

The cashier at your grocery store is helping provide your family with food—an important need. The auto mechanic who repairs your car meets a need. Because the people doing these jobs meet people's needs, their jobs can be ministries.

Some jobs, though, don't meet people's needs. Manufacturing cigarettes, for example, meets no legitimate need, and the product causes widespread suffering and death. No matter how socially respectable a job may be, if it does not help provide a service or product that meets people's needs, it is not ministry.

Test No. 2: Do you have a servant spirit?

For a job to be Christian ministry, though, it is not

enough that it meet a need. It must also be motivated by servanthood.

When Melody, Eddy's wife, was in the hospital for the birth of their fourth child, she felt surrounded by God's care. This was due in no small part to the ministry of compassionate Christian nurses. One nurse, though, did not want to be there. She came into the room complaining that she had been called in. She complained about what floor she had been assigned to. She performed her duties but never had a pleasant word for the patient. For her, taking care of Melody was not an opportunity to serve; it was just a job. Melody did not feel ministered to by that nurse.

A servant spirit can transform any useful job into a ministry. If a bank's computer programmer approaches his work not just as a way to earn a paycheck or increase the bank's profits, but as a way to serve the bank's customers with fast, accurate, dependable service—something we all need—the job can become a ministry, even if he never meets the customers. Being motivated by God's love for others is what makes the difference.

Whenever a Christian works with a caring commitment to serve those to whom he or she is providing needed goods or services, the work itself becomes more than a job; it is transformed into ministry.

Who is it you're serving?

When you work—whether at home, in an office, or in the cab of an 18-wheeler—who is it you are serving? Whose needs are you meeting by the product or service you help to provide? If you can answer that question, you are halfway toward having a ministry job rather than a secular job.

To go the other half of the way, you simply have to do your work *for* those people. Your goal, as you work, is to serve them, to meet their needs.

I (Eddy) heard of one Christian builder who prays for the family that will live in the home he is building. A quilter prays for the family that will spend cold nights snuggled under her quilt. These workers have found a way to remind themselves who it is they are serving. As they work, they are inspired by the fact that their work will minister to specific people, people they have not yet met. Not only are they lovingly preparing a house and a quilt for their future owners, but by their prayers they are releasing God's blessing into the lives of those they serve.

Remembering who it is you are serving can turn ordinary tasks into ministry. One mom we know confesses that when her baby demands to be held, she is tempted to feel she is wasting time. As she rocks her baby, she is not getting lunch cooked. She is not getting the laundry done.

But one day as she was impatiently rocking her baby, she remembered the last line of a magazine article she had read. It said, "A baby needs to be held when a baby needs to be held." That line reminded her that she was engaged in one of the most important ministries in the world—showing love to her child. She was then able to relax and concentrate on "doing love," confident there was no better way to invest her time.

How can you remind yourself of who it is you are serving with your work? Put a picture of a representative customer on the wall above your desk. Pray for the person who will receive each package you ship out of the shipping room. Offer a warm smile and a kind word to each customer you wait on. Whatever it is, allow a vision of the people you serve through your work to inspire you to add the secret ingredient of love to every task. When love for those you serve inspires your daily work, your work has become ministry.

No Christian should do "secular" work—work that is not holy or sacred. Every Christian's work, whether paid or unpaid, done at home or the office or the factory, is to be done to glorify God and serve other people.

Beyond the job description

Approaching your work with a servant spirit can transform any worthwhile task into ministry. But your work presents you with more opportunities for ministry than that—opportunities that go beyond your job description.

Mark, the insurance agent you met in chapter 1, has always tried to give his clients reliable, conscientious service. Because he brings a servant spirit to his job, working for the purpose of meeting his clients' needs, he ministers every day by doing what he is paid to do.

But after a few years in the business, Mark realized he had been overlooking some important ministry opportunities. He was struck, for example, with how many of his clients called to have their insurance policies changed due to divorce. Some would call to find out how their insurance rates would be affected if they followed through with a divorce they were considering.

Mark began to think about how these people needed a lot more than insurance quotes. They needed new hope for their marriages. So when these people called, he would give them the figures they asked for; then, if it seemed appropriate, he would express his concern. Sometimes he would say, "I'll be praying for you." To some he would recommend a book or a video that had helped him in his marriage, or refer the couple to his church's counseling service. "I know of three couples whose marriages have been saved because they followed through on what I suggested to them," Mark says.

During the past year, Mark has become more intentional about sharing his faith with people he contacts through his job. He realizes that however sensitive he may try to be in doing this, he still runs a risk of offending some people, and he may lose business if someone is offended. "But," Mark says, "I've decided that sometimes I've got to stick my neck out and take that risk.

"Not long ago a man who was going through some hard times called to set up an appointment to talk about his insurance. Because his life-style was so obviously different from mine, I thought, If anyone would be offended at my sharing my faith, this guy would. But when I woke up on the morning of our appointment, I sensed the Holy Spirit saying, 'I'm going to give you the chance to talk with him about spiritual things.'

"When I met with him later that day, I did get to tell him how God could help him with his problems. He said, 'I can't believe this. You're the third or fourth person to say that to me this week.' Before he left my office that day, he'd let me pray with him."

What kinds of opportunities for ministry does your work offer you—above and beyond the basic requirements of your job? What spiritual needs do you see in those you contact through your work? What emotional needs? What needs for practical help? What financial needs? How can you respond to these needs in ways that demonstrate God's love?

Am I in the right job?

Most of us, as we come to more deeply understand that we are called to minister through our work, will wonder, Is the job I have the best place I can live out God's good news, or could I have a greater ministry in some other kind of work? It's a good question and an important one.

When you ask yourself this question, either one of two things is true, according to Pastor Gordon Cosby. "Your dissatisfaction is God's instruction to learn to do every task to his glory, or it is God calling you to cast your nets in another place. If it is the first, there will be the contentment of consecrated work; if it is the latter, the dissatisfaction will persist."[1]

What may be the best possible setting for ministry for one person, as the insurance business seems to be for Mark, will not be at all right for another person with a different personality, interests, and spiritual gifts. While it is not always easy to know what kind of work God is calling us to—or even what role He wants us to take in our churches, families, or communities—it is possible for each of us to learn to recognize His call. In the next chapter, we will look at how to do just that.

*Where do you mourn with Jesus for the pain
in the world? What would give you joy
in this painful situation?
Where the world's deep pain and your deep joy
intersect, there you find your call.*

5

DISCOVERING YOUR CALL

"The church has forgotten me; nobody cares," an elderly shut-in told his pastor. Bob Martin was moved by this man's story when the pastor repeated it in church the next Sunday. After the service Bob asked his pastor for the man's name and address.

Walter Gooden, Bob learned, was 80 years old. His only family was an older brother, who seldom visited. He had no one in the world who cared about him.

Over the next two years Walter's house became a regular stop for Bob. They sat around and talked a lot, went to the grocery store together, went to doctor's appointments together. When Walter was moved to a nursing home, Bob kept visiting him, and when Walter went to the hospital, Bob was there. Shortly after Bob moved away from Wichita, Kans., he was called back to attend Walter's funeral.

After his move to Oklahoma City, Bob had a similar experience with an elderly lady. He went to see her every day and took her lunch on Sundays. After a man beat her and tried to rape her, Bob was there to comfort her.

Bob says, "The Lord used these two experiences to burden my heart for compassionate ministries." Today Bob leads his church's Compassionate Ministries team in reaching out to a growing number of needs like these.

It is important for each of us to discover the ministries

God is calling us to. If we try to do a little of everything, we'll end up doing nothing well. Just as each part of the human body has certain functions, so God has given each member of the Body of Christ specific jobs to do. The only way the Body can work as God intends is for each member to do his or her own job well.

How can we know what ministries God wants us to do? One pastor advises his members, "If God has burdened you about a particular need in a person's life and you are able to meet that need and minister to that person . . . , then proceed prayerfully and thoughtfully."[1] Bob's first step in discovering his ministry was simply responding to a single person's need, for which God had burdened him. It is only as we reach out to meet needs that our spiritual gifts can emerge and our calls be clarified.

Congratulations! You're gifted!

Knowing what your spiritual gift is can sometimes help you make wiser ministry decisions. When Paul wrote the Corinthians and Romans, he assumed they already knew what their spiritual gifts were; and, in his letter to the Romans, he gave specific instructions to each on how to use his or her gift (12:6-8). So Paul saw practical value in Christians knowing what their gifts were.

Sometimes, though, trying to identify our spiritual gifts can be frustrating. The Bible does not define all the spiritual gifts; it just lists them. So, different scholars have come up with sometimes vastly different definitions. What we end up calling our gifts may depend on which spiritual gifts book we happen to be reading or which "spiritual gifts test" we have just taken.

But the lack of agreement on definitions does not mean we cannot identify our gifts. It only means we should not be too concerned about matching the "correct" label with each person's gift. What really matters is that we clearly identify the special ministry abilities God has given us.

Bob Martin, for example, identifies his gift this way: "God has gifted me to reach out and touch a hurt." Bob's spiritual gift is probably what the Bible calls "showing mercy" (Rom. 12:8). He may sometimes refer to his gift that way. But if he finds it more helpful to call his gift "showing compassion" or "reaching out and touching hurts," there's no reason he should not use the name that describes the gift most clearly for him.

Sometimes spiritual gifts and talents are confused. While both are gifts from God and often work hand in hand, God has given all people talents. Spiritual gifts operate only through believers, those in whom God's Spirit lives.

A talent is a skill like painting or writing. A spiritual gift is an ability to allow God's Spirit to touch the spirit of another person through you in a particular way.

For example, singing is a talent. Many non-Christians are good singers. But a Christian who ministers through singing is not only using a talent but also exercising a spiritual gift. That gift may be encouragement, teaching, or even prophecy, depending on what effect the ministry has on the spirits of those who hear.

While you do not have to identify your spiritual gift before you can minister, knowing what your gift is can help you make better-informed decisions about where and how to minister. How, then, can you identify your spiritual gift?

A gift is visible only when it is in action. As you respond in love to those needs for which God is giving you a special concern, as Bob Martin did, your gift will emerge. People respond to identical needs in different ways, depending on what gifts God has given them. It is only as you respond in ministry that the special ministry abilities God has given you become clear.

What is a call?

Our spiritual gifts and our calls to ministry are related, but different. First Cor. 12:4-5 reads, "There are different kinds of gifts, but the same Spirit. There are different kinds of service, but the same Lord." Just as there are different spiritual gifts, there are different kinds of service or ministries in which we can use those gifts.

One way the Bible uses the word *call* is to describe God's call to salvation that comes to everyone. We also talk about how all of us are called to be ministers. But in this chapter we are focusing on yet a third meaning of call, on God's call to a particular ministry or kind of service.

God called Moses at the burning bush to deliver His people from Egyptian slavery. On the Damascus road, God called Saul to be a witness to the Gentiles. Today God calls some to pastoral ministry, evangelism, or missionary work. But God's call comes not only to those people in the professional ministry but to all of us.

And it may come not just once but several times during our lives. While some spiritual gifts can be expected to operate for a lifetime, calls to specific kinds of minstry can change. Many of us will be given different missions for different stages of our lives.

How can you know what kind of ministry God is calling you to do for this period of your life?

What causes you pain?

Our own pain can point us to what God is calling us to do. In 1991 Dillard Taylor started a ministry called JobNet, a support group for unemployed and underemployed people. Where did he get the idea? After 23 years of continuous employment, he suddenly found himself out of work and in need of practical support. His own pain sensitized him to the needs of others in similar situations.

God's call may come to us, not through our own pain,

but through the need of another. A medical doctor in Newton, Kans., aware that many people in his community could not afford health insurance, organized a low-cost clinic. A black pastor in Jackson, Miss., in response to the substandard housing in which many people in his community lived, launched a housing rehabilitation program. You can probably think of ministries in your own community, perhaps even in your own congregation, that have come into being because someone felt the pain of another.

The Church of the Saviour in Washington, D.C., asks two questions to help people clarify their calls. The first is *Where do you mourn with Jesus for the pain in the world?* Where in your world is the pain you most long to heal? Is it the pain of homelessness? Of latchkey children? Of racism? Are you burdened about teens who are growing up without a strong commitment to God? Or by the woundedness of adults you know who were abused as children? Is your heart broken by the unhealthy marriages you see? Or do you mourn your church's limited vision for world missions or its failure to include the poor in congregational life?

The pain or frustration that most deeply moves your spirit likely points to your call.

What gives you joy?

The second question the Church of the Saviour asks is *What would give you joy in this painful situation?* What is the better world you dream of in relation to this problem? Is it a world in which the homeless of your city all have decent shelter and food? A world where the racial groups in your town work together to understand one another and achieve common goals? Is it a world where those in your town with troubled marriages can find support, acceptance, and practical help in healing their relationships? Are you burdened for the many unsaved persons around you who need the good news of Christ? Where the world's deep pain and your deep joy intersect, there you find your call.

Another way to ask this question is "If you had unlimited resources, what would you dream of doing about this pain?" Even if you have identified the pain that calls you, it may not be self-evident how to respond. It is important to take time to hear from God so that when you do act, you will know you have been sent.

The call inward

When our family was ministering in the inner city, I (Eddy) had a strong sense of call that gave my work focus and tremendous energy. Melody, my wife, did not share that sense of call. I often tried to help her identify her call, but my attempts to help would only make her feel more frustrated and more guilty that she did not know what her call was.

Then Melody went on a spiritual retreat—the same kind of retreat that had so helped me clarify my call. What she told me when she got back was hardly what I had expected. The retreat leader had told Melody she did not need a call. She recognized that Melody was burned out, emotionally exhausted from trying to minister. What she needed to do was take care of herself. "Once you're well enough," the retreat leader had said, "a call will come."

That was the first time I realized that there are periods in our lives when God calls us to focus, not on outward mission, but on our own healing. We may need to take time, for example, to grieve, to overcome an addiction, or to recover from the effects of abuse. Healing is hard work and, in its most intense stages, demands most of our energy. During those times we need to focus on the healing work without feeling guilty that we have little or no energy for outward mission.

God may also call us away from ministry for times of renewal. And, like Paul, who spent three years in Arabia after his conversion before beginning his public ministry (Gal. 1:17-18), there may be periods when our focus is not on ministering in the present, but on preparing for ministry in the future.

When God calls us inward, we need to obey that call, and we need to support others who are called to work on the renewal, healing, or preparation of their spirits for future ministry. Once the intense inner work is completed, a call to outward ministry will come.

Try on a ministry

Discovering your call is seldom cut and dried. It usually involves experimenting. If a ministry opportunity comes your way and you don't know if you have the gifts needed to do it, you don't have to be sure you will succeed in it before you give it a try. If, after praying about it, you feel drawn to respond to the need, you can "try on" the ministry for a while to test whether it is a good match for you.

When Shirley Posey was asked to teach an adult Sunday School class, she doubted that teaching was the right place for her. She had taught high school English for several years but had not felt she had done a very good job. But the Sunday School class had been without a teacher for quite a while, and attendance was dropping. So, after praying about it, Shirley agreed to give it a try.

To her surprise, Shirley found she enjoyed studying and preparing her Sunday School lessons. "It was the best thing that ever happened to me," she said. "It forced me to study the Word and memorize it. It prepared me for hard things to come in my life." Not only did she enjoy teaching on Sunday mornings, but also she loved being involved in the lives of her class members, "pastoring" them seven days a week. People responded positively to her ministry, and attendance grew.

Through this process, Shirley says, "I discovered teaching was my spiritual gift." If she hadn't been willing to experiment, Shirley might never have found her gift.

How gifts are confirmed

When you "try on a ministry," one of two things happens. If you have a gift in that area, the church body sees the gift operating and affirms it. If you are not gifted in that area, your experiment is still a success because you have learned something about yourself. You can then keep "trying on" other ministries until you find one that uses your gifts.

Shirley has been teaching her Sunday School class for 20 years now. During that time it has grown from 24 adults to about 100. But the clearest evidence that Shirley is where she belongs is not in how many come to hear her teach, but in the lives God has touched through her ministry.

Phil and Ann, charter members of the class, describe how Shirley and her husband, James, supported them through a divorce, then nurtured them each individually after the divorce and helped them learn to communicate with each other about the real issues in their relationship. Eventually they were able to remarry. Ann says, "We both know the Holy Spirit used James and Shirley to reach out to us, wrapped His arms around all of us, and drew us back to Him and to each other."

Rowena, who joined the class seven years ago, explains what Shirley's ministry has meant to her: "I was not really interested in Sunday School, but I was convinced by a coworker to attend Shirley Posey's class. I saw that the faces of those in her class had such wonderful, peaceful expressions of love. I asked Shirley how I could get what those in her class had. For the next two years she met with me once a week to disciple me. She helped me learn the importance of staying in the Word. I learned how obedience and prayer could change a life. Shirley truly got me moving in the right direction in my spiritual life."

These and many other changed lives confirm that Shirley has the gifts needed for her present ministry.

Gifts and call are also confirmed in a second way—by the joy experienced by the one ministering. "This class has given my life meaning," says Shirley. "It gives me something to get up for and look forward to every day. I've gotten tired sometimes and have wanted time off, but I have never wanted to quit."

The genius of team ministry

Many acts of ministry are spontaneous responses to needs we encounter during the day. But obeying a call usually involves a major commitment to a specific kind of ministry over a period of years. None of us alone has all the gifts needed for a major long-term ministry, but when gifts are blended, new possibilities for ministry are created. When people minister as a team, they can support and encourage one another, and work can be shared, so that no one is overburdened.

How are ministry teams formed? Some can be formed simply by bringing together people already involved in similar ministries. For example, the director of children's ministries in your church might host in her home monthly meetings for all the children's Sunday School teachers. At these gatherings, the director could outline her vision for the church's ministry to children, and teachers could share what they felt called to do. Teachers could discuss problems and work out solutions and make programming and curriculum decisions together. They could mention students with special needs and pray for their students and each other.

Ministry teams can be created for any part of the church's life that involves two or more people in ministry—music or visitation, ministry to teens or to senior adults.

Ministry teams can also take the form of support groups for ministries of the church scattered. For example, if three couples in the church are foster parents, those six people could get together regularly to share joys and pains, questions and learnings, and to encourage and pray for one another. They might also work out practical ways to support each other, such as trading off child care to give each other time off. Or a group of business executives might get together weekly over lunch to discuss ways they can transform their jobs into ministries and to hold each other accountable for following through with ministry goals and spiritual disciplines.

Sounding a call

Then, of course, a ministry team can be formed to start a new ministry. The Church of the Saviour in Washington, D.C., invites members who believe God may be giving them a vision for a new ministry to first test the call with church leaders, then to "sound a call" to the rest of the church body. This sounding of call may take the form of a printed handout describing the vision, or a talk given in a worship service. Other churches do this with announcement sheets, newsletters, or interviews during services. Once the call is sounded, others in the congregation are invited to consider whether God is calling them to that same ministry. Whenever two or more people are called to the same ministry, a ministry team is formed.

However we do it, we need to connect with others within our own congregations, and in some cases from other congregations, whom God is calling to the same ministry to which He is calling us. Only as we minister together is the power of body life released into our ministries.

As we respond in compassion to needs God brings across our paths, our gifts become active. As we name our gifts, our ministries take on clearer focus. As we find the point where the world's deep pain and our deep joy inter-sect, we discover call. And as we join with others who share our call and whose gifts complement ours, we are forged into ministry teams through which God's power and love can flow to heal a hurting world.

As more and more people join together in obeying God's call, the result will be nothing short of a revolution. In fact, as the next chapter shows, the revolution has already begun.

*Forty years ago Elton Trueblood wrote,
"If the average church should suddenly
take seriously the notion that every
laymember—man or woman—is
really a minister of Christ, we could have
something like a revolution in a very short
time."[1] Today, in church after church,
his prediction is coming true.*

6

A QUIET REVOLUTION

One Sunday two Cambodian junior high girls rode the Sunday School bus to Long Beach, Calif., First Church of the Nazarene. In the weeks that followed, other Cambodian children joined them.

One Sunday School teacher, Letha George, thought, "Here's a people that are sending their children to church, but if I don't do something to get the parents, I'll never keep the children."[2] So she sent letters home with the children inviting their parents to Sunday School.

The next Sunday five women came. A few weeks later men started coming too. When the adult class for Cambodians grew to 20 or 25, Letha wondered, What have I done? These people here at church may run me off!

But Long Beach was not that kind of church. Other members volunteered to work with the Southeast Asians, and within months the ministry had mushroomed into three large classes, one each for adults, youth, and children.

John and Mildred Schmidt, a retired couple who had been active in the congregation since 1922, saw how much the Cambodians wanted and needed to learn English. They volunteered to go into the Asian community to teach English as a second language, often using the English Bible as a text. Sometimes, as they took students home after a study session or a social event, John and Mildred had the opportunity to lead them to Christ. Many more young people accepted Christ during the actual class sessions.

Long Beach Nazarenes got involved in many ways, from bus ministry outreach to holding citizenship classes to moving furniture for Cambodian families to helping them find jobs. By the time John Calhoun came as senior pastor, over 300 Cambodians were attending services each week. Glenn and Letha George were leading a large adult Sunday School class and conducting multilingual Sunday morning worship services in the church's fellowship hall. Today some of the Cambodian men testify that they are Christians more because of Glenn's broad smile, warm handshakes, and his arm so often wrapped around their shoulders, than because of the preaching.

The Asian church kept growing, and it soon became clear they needed a facility of their own. Though it meant delaying the expansion of their own facility, Long Beach First Church made their financial reserves available to enable the Cambodians to buy their own building. On February 23, 1986, a building in the heart of the Asian community was dedicated, with almost 900 people crammed into a sanctuary designed for 450.

This facility is now the meeting place of two congregations—one speaking the Khmer language and the other a Lao dialect—that make up the New Life Church of the Nazarene. In addition to hosting 600 worshipers each week, this building also houses the Asian Nazarene Bible College Extension. Here Southeast Asian Nazarenes prepare for ministry leadership, not only among refugees, but also in their homelands, to which God is leading some to return.

Ung Ty, for example, came to Christ through the outreach of New Life Church and eventually became pastor of the Khmer congregation. In 1992 he and his wife returned to Cambodia as Nazarene missionaries. Each week over a thousand people gather to worship at the Phnom Penh Church of the Nazarene. New Life's ministry has also led to the birth of an Asian church in Visalia, Calif., and both Khmer- and Lao-speaking congregations in Modesto, Calif.

Long Beach First Church's Asian outreach has brought new life not only to hundreds of Cambodians but also to the parent congregation, especially the lay members who have ministered among the Cambodians week after week. Volunteer Ruth Anderson says, "I had hoped I might find some way to minister to the people of New Life. What I discovered was that their ministry to me gave me *new life*. They have shown me a love I've rarely experienced."

A revolution in Oklahoma

In 1989 First Church of the Nazarene in Bethany, Okla., was in the midst of what they called a "Fifty-Day Spiritual Adventure" leading up to Easter. During this time the pastor's sermons all focused on bringing Christ's hope to the surrounding community. Hundreds of members committed themselves to five spiritual disciplines, including keeping a spiritual journal and reading the Christian classic *In His Steps*. As members began taking seriously the question posed by the book, "What would Jesus do?" it became clear that the Holy Spirit was doing something special in many of their lives.

"We knew it wouldn't be right to just end the 50 days, then return to church as usual," said Dave McKellips, associate pastor. "People were being renewed, revived, and they needed to respond." The church provided a way.

At the end of the 50 days, members were asked to name needs they saw in the community to which they felt God might want the church to reach out. Suggestions were sorted into 13 areas. Then on April 2, the Sunday after Easter, a bulletin insert listed these 13 areas of potential ministry and extended the following invitation: "Look

over the list of ministry groups, find the one that most interests you, and go to the corresponding room at 5 P.M.
tonight."

The insert listed four community ministries already in
progress—a ministry to the elderly, a prison ministry, a
Meals on Wheels program, and a ministry with the chemi-
cally dependent and their families. It also listed nine possible new ministries that had been suggested by members,
including ministry with the hearing impaired, ministry with
the hungry and homeless, and a tutoring ministry with
adults. The insert explained that a new Community
Ministry Group would be started for each area in which
four or more people were willing to get involved.

Lay ministry is nothing new at Bethany First Church.
The congregation has a long history of strong and distin-
guished lay leadership. But the Holy Spirit was up to something new that spring, and people were offered a new way
to respond. Rather than new ministries having to be
approved by various committees and boards and then operated under their direction, laypeople were turned loose to
start grass roots groups. While church staff would eagerly
encourage and support these ministries, ownership and
leadership would rest with those to whom God had given
the specific vision and calling.

The pastoral staff also made clear that every group had
permission to fail. Groups did not have to wait until they
had so many volunteers and resources that they felt assured
of success before they started. In fact, it was to be expected
that while some groups would develop long-term ministries, others would experiment with a new outreach for a
while, only to discover that they didn't have the right com-
bination of resources to make it work. And that was OK.

With this freedom to risk, the people of Bethany First
Church began to dream new dreams and experiment with

new ministries. Some of those original Community Ministry Groups are still going strong today. Others have dissolved. Yet others have arisen as God continues to plant vision in the hearts of people throughout the congregation. Excerpts from the church's Community Ministries newsletter highlight the varied ways people are touching their community with God's love.

Ten months ago the Bethany First Church RAIN (Regional AIDS Interfaith Network) Team was assigned their first client. We were not sure how we were going to react to Mike or how he was going to react to us, but we were committed to represent the love of Jesus to this young man during the final stages of his life.

Last week we, as a team, attended Mike's funeral. Mike had become a friend to all of us. We were given not only the opportunity to serve Mike in a variety of ways but also the special privilege of walking hand in hand with him to death's door. I believe all of us on the RAIN team would readily admit that we received much more than we gave during the 10 months we cared for Mike.

* * *

The unemployment support group has formed at Bethany First Church and meets weekly every Sunday at 4:45 P.M. If you have found yourself out of work, know someone who is, or are just interested in learning more about how to deal with that possibility, call Dillard Taylor or stop by and join in.

* * *

Linda Shaw has been heading up a wonderful ministry at Mabel Bassett [a women's prison] for the past two years. Between 20 and 25 women regularly attend the Bible study.

Another group holds regular worship services at various correctional institutions [for men] around the state and have done so for several years. If you are interested in joining them, contact Lloyd Keith.

* * *

"Two years ago I began to look for ways I could contribute to our compassionate ministries program. A black sign-up book for Meals on Wheels was passed around our Sunday School class. This seemed like a way to help without having to find a baby-sitter for my two children. The three of us set out only to deliver meals to the elderly but came home with a book of poetry, homemade bread, and more hugs than we could count."

* * *

Volunteer teams are forming to renovate the two remaining apartment units at Bethlehem Transitional Shelter for Homeless Families. Bob Martin has volunteered to serve as coordinator. Volunteers are not required to have any special skills or tools.

* * *

Looking for a different Friday night experience? Every fifth Friday (four times a year) we have a Nazarene Night at the City Rescue Mission. We have lots of singing and a short message from the Bible. There are always people to pray with. If the joy of service isn't enough, we always go out for pizza afterward!

Senior Pastor Melvin McCullough identifies two lessons he learned from witnessing the renewal at Bethany First Church that gave birth to many of these ministries.

"First, I learned that in spiritual renewal not only can the Holy Spirit use an anointed evangelist or concerned pastor who has a vision for revival, but He can use perhaps even more powerfully the personal testimonies of laypeople who have been genuinely revitalized.

"Second, the hundreds of people who received new spiritual energy recognized immediately that they needed an outlet for service and social action that would penetrate the community around us. It has been one of the most meaningful experiences of my pastoral ministry to observe a spiritual awakening that bears such observable fruit in transforming the culture and the community."

A revolution in Ontario

In 1989 the Brampton, Ont., Church of the Nazarene redefined Pastor Reg Graves's job description, directing him to focus his time and energy in three areas: preaching, crisis visitation, and supporting the ministry of several lay pastors whom he would appoint, subject to board approval. All his other responsibilities would be assigned to lay pastors and teams of laypeople who would work with them.

Brampton now has seven lay pastors, each responsible for one area of the church's life—stewardship, small groups, missions, children's ministries, outreach, visitation, or music. An eighth area, youth ministry, was led by lay pastors until it became necessary to hire a full-time youth pastor.

As new people come into the congregation, they are invited to participate in a class, offered three times a year, on discovering their spiritual gifts. They are then each encouraged to become involved in one of the congregation's eight areas of ministry.

Members are clear about where ministry responsibilities lie. When a problem arises in children's ministries, for example, it is not taken to Pastor Graves, but to the lay pastor for children's ministries. And the pastor no longer attends so many committee meetings. Finance committee meetings, for example, are handled by the lay pastor for stewardship.

Since the first lay pastor was appointed three years ago, the church has grown from 160 to 250. To minister to the needs of the growing congregation, more lay pastors are appointed as needed. The church soon plans to add a lay pastor for prayer and a lay pastor for administration.

How does Pastor Graves feel about his new role? "I

admit that some things have been difficult for me to give up," he says, "but overall these years have been the most rewarding I've ever had as a pastor. I've been freed up to do the things I do best and enjoy the most."

Not only has Pastor Graves been freed to concentrate on what he does best, but also laypeople at Brampton Church of the Nazarene have been empowered to minister as never before, and more and more lives are being touched by God's love through the congregation.

Marjorie Osborne's hands were in her kitchen sink in Toronto one day when the Lord planted the thought in her mind: "There's going to be a big change in your life." She had no idea what God was talking about.

Then at the 1985 Nazarene General Assembly in Anaheim, Calif., no matter what service she was attending, no matter who the speaker was or what the topic was, she kept hearing the Lord say to her, "Ten thousand Canadian Nazarenes are not enough." Though Marjorie had no idea what God wanted her to do about this, during the big Communion service on Sunday morning she gave God her response: "I'll give the rest of my life to changing that if You'll show me how."

Marjorie had been home from General Assembly only three days when the Rosewood Church of the Nazarene in Toronto called, asking her to be their church planting director. She really didn't know if she had the necessary gifts or skills. She had been a stay-at-home wife and mother for 25 years. But God's call had been so clear in Anaheim that Marjorie had no doubt what her answer should be.

At Rosewood, Marjorie guided the planting of both a Chinese church and an Anglo church. She went on to coordinate a church-planting program for her district and is now the church growth coordinator for the Church of the Nazarene in Canada. Marjorie has been personally involved in over 30 church plants in Canada, and in the past few years the number of Nazarene churches in the Toronto area has grown from 14 to 37.

A revolution around the world

In the Church of the Nazarene in Tuxtla, Mexico—Templo Cristiano de Tuxtla—congregational life has been divided into 10 areas, and lay leaders have been appointed to direct each of these areas of ministry. God has been adding many new believers to the church as new ministries have been launched and existing ministries extended.

Since 1980, the Church of the Nazarene in South America has grown from 19,000 members to more than 80,000 members. What accounts for such phenomenal growth? "We are working to involve all believers in winning others," writes Louie Bustle, the regional director for the Church of the Nazarene in South America. "We have changed a paternalistic mentality, giving authority and responsibility to all who are willing to be involved in impacting our continent. Since we believe that 'God does not show favoritism' (Acts 10:34), we have mobilized all our people regardless of their education, income, or nationality."[3]

Will you join the revolution?

Never before have so many nations and peoples been so open to the good news of Christ. Never before have there been so many opportunities for ministry. And never before have there been so many people with so many spiritual, emotional, and physical needs. In this day of accelerating change, we can be sure the future will continue to bring both increasing need as well as increasing opportunities for ministry.

If the church is to fulfill its mission in this time of soaring need, we laypeople cannot sit back and leave ministry to the ministry professionals. We must say yes to God's call and join with our pastors and other leaders in forming a dynamic ministry partnership.

During World War II a statue of Christ that stood at the center of a small French village was shattered in the fighting. Villagers carefully saved the pieces until the war was over, then rebuilt the statue. Once it had been reassembled, though, the people found that Christ's hands were missing. They weren't sure what to do. Should they leave the incomplete statue up, or should they take it down? It was only when someone placed a small hand-painted sign at the statue's base that the villagers were able to agree that the statue was in fact complete and that it should stand. The sign read, "Christ has no hands but ours."

Are you willing to commit the rest of your life to being Christ's hands in a broken world? God wants to use you—not someday, but right now. God wants to use you—not sometime, but all the time. God wants to use you—not somewhere, but right where you are.

After all, ministry isn't just for ministers. On second thought, though, ministry is just for ministers, for God has called you and me and every other believer to be His ministers and has entrusted us with His mission. If we don't do it, no one will. Christ has no hands but ours.

Will you join the revolution?

NOTES

Foreword

1. C. Peter Wagner, *Your Church Can Grow* (Ventura, Calif.: Regal Books, 1984), 77.

Chapter 1

1. R. Paul Stevens, *Liberating the Laity* (Downers Grove, Ill.: InterVarsity Press, 1985), 40-41.

2. Elizabeth O'Connor, *Call to Commitment* (New York: Harper and Row, 1963), 102-3.

3. James Garlow, *Partners in Ministry* (Kansas City: Beacon Hill Press of Kansas City, 1981), 61.

4. Ibid., 63.

5. Richard Wilke, *And Are We Yet Alive?* (Nashville: Abingdon Press, 1986), 85.

Chapter 2

1. C. Peter Wagner, ed., with Win Arn and Elmer Towns, *Church Growth—State of the Art* (Wheaton, Ill.: Tyndale House Publishers, 1986), 109.

Chapter 3

1. James Garlow, *Partners in Ministry* (Kansas City: Beacon Hill Press of Kansas City, 1987), video tape recording.

2. Adapted from a talk by Jim Couchenour given at Canton, Ohio, First Church of the Nazarene, August 27, 1989.

3. Ibid.

4. Garlow, *Partners in Ministry*, 139.

Chapter 4

1. O'Connor, *Call to Commitment*, 169.

Chapter 5

1. Gib Martin, in Lawrence O. Richards and Clyde Hoeldtke, *A Theology of Church Leadership* (Grand Rapids: Zondervan Publishing House, 1980), 258.

Chapter 6

1. Elton Trueblood, *Your Other Vocation* (New York: Harper and Brothers, 1952), 9.

2. A. Brent Cobb, *Hasten the Harvest* (Kansas City: Beacon Hill Press of Kansas City, 1988), 73. Most of this story of the Asian outreach of the Long Beach First Church of the Nazarene is adapted from this book.

3. Louie E. Bustle and Bruno Radi, *New Solutions* (Nashville: Choice Publishing, 1992), 19.

LEADER'S
GUIDE

How to Use This
LEADER'S GUIDE

A note to pastors and lay leaders

If you dream of mobilizing and equipping all the people of your congregation for ministry, this book was written with you and your people in mind. While we hope the book will help all who read it, we believe it will have its greatest impact when used for its primary purpose—as a tool to stimulate congregational renewal. If as many as 20% of the adults in your church will complete this study and then act on what they have learned, it could well prove to be a watershed event in your congregation's history.

This leader's guide gives detailed, activity-by-activity instructions for six sessions, each 45 minutes to an hour long. Sessions include discussion, reading of Scripture and stories, and sharing and prayer in small groups—but no lecture. Because the lesson plans are so complete, the leader should need to spend only an hour or so preparing for each session.

Possible settings

This course lends itself to various settings. It can be a congregation-wide study held during six consecutive Wednesday or Sunday evening services. One church offered it as an optional class before the Sunday evening service. Another church held a churchwide study of lay ministry as a creative alternative to their usual fall revival, meeting each weeknight during one week, climaxing Sunday morning. Or your church might build an all-church weekend retreat around this study.

It can also be used with smaller groups. You could offer the class as an adult Sunday School elective. Existing small groups might study this in their regular meetings. It could even be used as the basis for a church leadership retreat for board members and their spouses.

Most who complete this study will emerge from it with a

broader understanding of ministry and greater vision for the future of the church. So the more who participate in the study, the greater the likelihood that a "critical mass" of laypeople will become catalysts to create a new level of ministry consciousness throughout the congregation.

Who should teach it?

The pastor may want to lead this study to register his strong commitment to each layperson's ministry. On the other hand, if a layperson leads it, the teacher is not only talking about but also modeling lay ministry. One good option might be for a pastor and layperson to teach the class together, demonstrating the pastor's support and modeling not only lay leadership but ministry partnership as well.

More important than whether the study leader is a pastor or layperson are the skills of the teacher. Look for a teacher who knows how to lead lively, interesting class discussions. Do not choose a teacher who tends toward a lecture style. The ability to lecture well is a wonderful gift, but it is not one needed for this study.

Adapt to your needs

These sessions have been field-tested with a group of 20 to 30 laypeople in a Nazarene church to make sure the teaching methods described really work. While we hope you find the described learning activities helpful, don't feel limited by them. Change the teaching plans however you need to, to make the sessions work better for your group.

Using the text

Each person or couple in your group should have a copy of this text. The text will often be used in class, and, hopefully, each participant will read each chapter in full prior to the class. No session, however, depends on participants' having read the chapter before class. In fact, this leader's guide is unusual in that each session is intended to *introduce* a chapter, not to build on the participants' study of it. That means that at your first meeting, for example, you will distribute copies of the book, lead your group through session 1, *then* suggest participants read chapter 1 when they get home. The idea is to so intrigue your group members with the session's topic that they will want to learn more when they leave the session.

Because of this structure, visitors to your sessions should be able to participate fully in all activities.

After the study

Since the study's purpose is to mobilize the members of your church for ministry, the course will be a failure if people merely come, learn, enjoy, then go on as they always have. How can those who are ready to move out in new ministry initiatives be supported? How can those already involved in ministry be brought together in teams?

A pastor should closely monitor the progress of the class and be prepared to propose specific ways participants can implement what they have learned about ministry and their own calls. This may involve creating new structures for team ministry. (See the last two sections of chapter 5 and sessions 5 and 6 of the leader's guide.) Unless people have practical ways to translate into action what they've learned, the study will likely be a wasted effort. But if it is used as a springboard to launch people into greater ministry, it may prove to be a turning point for the congregation.

SESSION 1
THE MINISTRY MYTH

> **SESSION GOAL**
> *To enable each believer present to recognize and affirm that God has called him or her to be a minister.*

Materials and advance preparation needed
1. Paper and pencil for each participant
2. Chalkboard or newsprint and marker
3. Before the session, ask two people to be prepared to read from chapter 1, one to read Gary's story (from the beginning of the chapter up to the first subhead) and one to read Mark's story (which begins with the second paragraph under "The high cost of the myth").
4. Bibles

ACTIVITY 1 (5-10 min.)

Why Am I Here?

   If the members of this group have come together specifically to explore lay ministry, a great place to begin is to invite them to tell why they have come. Some may have come just out of curiosity, but most probably have specific hopes or felt needs that have brought them to the session. You'll want to listen carefully to what people are hoping to receive from this study so that in the coming weeks you can emphasize those aspects of the study that speak to their concerns.

   If you are using this as curriculum in a Sunday School class or some other existing group, "Why are you here?" may not be the best question to begin with. Change it to **"What would you like to get out of this study?"**

If not all group members know each other, each should give his or her name before answering the question.

ACTIVITY 2 (5-10 min.)

Ministry Is . . .

Pass blank paper and a pencil to each person. Say, **"Do you remember the cartoons that would start out, 'Love is . . . ,' which would then be followed by a description of love and a cartoon to illustrate it? We're going to do the same thing, but with ministry. The important thing here isn't to produce impressive artwork; this is just an activity to help us start thinking about ministry. So across the top of your paper write: 'Ministry is . . .' Across the bottom of your paper finish that sentence, then draw a cartoon to illustrate your definition of ministry."**

Allow a minute or so for people to work, then ask them to share responses. Write answers on a chalkboard or newsprint that says at the top, "Ministry is . . ."

ACTIVITY 3 (10-15 min.)

The Ministry Myth

Say, **"Having a clear and biblical understanding of ministry is important, because misconceptions can cause confusion or even paralysis in our spiritual lives. I've asked a couple of people to read stories of people who paid a high price because they believed mistaken ideas about ministry."**

The two people you have recruited before class will now read Gary's and Mark's stories from chapter 1. After the stories are read, ask, **"Most of us have been frustrated about ministry at some time. Your frustrations may be similar to Mark's or Gary's, or they may be different. What frustrations do you experience in relation to ministry?"**

Once again, listen carefully for clues about what you are going to need to emphasize in your study in the coming weeks.

ACTIVITY 4 (8-10 min.)

Who Are the Ministers?
Ask for five volunteers to look up and be ready to read the following scriptures: 1 Pet. 4:10-11; Rom. 12:6-8; 1 Cor. 12:4-7; 1 Pet. 2:5, 9; Rev. 1:6.

Ask for the first three passages (through the 1 Corinthians passage) to be read; then ask the following questions:
1. **"To whom does the Holy Spirit give spiritual gifts?"** (All believers.)
2. **"What is their purpose?"** (Various answers are correct. The point you want to bring out is that they are gifts for ministry.)
3. **"Then who are the ministers?"** (All believers.)

Ask for the reading of the last two passages, but before they are read, ask the group members to listen for what key word each of the verses has in common. Once the verses have been read, ask:
4. **"What key word did these verses have in common?"** ("Priest.")
5. **"In the Old Testament, who were priests?"** (The Levites. The point to be made here is that it was only a select group. Not all people of faith were priests.)
6. **"According to these verses, who are priests today?"** (All believers.)

Explain briefly what it means to be a priest (see page 24).

Next, read Ephesians 4:11-12a from the *Revised Standard Version or New Revised Standard Version.* This is found in the text of chapter 1, and you can simply read it out of the book if you wish. The reason for using one of these versions is that they use the word "ministry." Some other versions use the word "service." If group members are comparing, you can point out that "service" and "ministry" are both translations of the same Greek word.

After reading this passage, ask:
7. **"According to this passage, why has God called certain people to roles of leadership in the church?"** ("To equip the saints for the work of ministry.")
8. **"Who then are the ministers?"** (All the saints, or

all God's people.)

9. **"Which group is to assist the other with ministry? Are the members called to assist the leaders with the ministry of the church, or are the leaders called to help the members with their ministries?"** (Leaders are called to equip the members with their ministries.) Optional follow-up question: **"Have we sometimes gotten this backward in our thinking?"**

10. **"So how many of us in here are called to be ministers?"** You might even ask for a show of hands. It might be good for some to raise their hands who have never before called themselves ministers.

ACTIVITY 5 (4-8 min.)

Ministries in Progress

This activity is optional, depending on time available. If you are down to only 10 minutes or so of time left, skip this and move on to Activity 6.

Say, **"Not only are all of us called to be ministers, but also most of us are already involved in ministry every day, even if we've never referred to those activities as ministries. What are you regularly involved in that you would consider ministry?"**

Likely answers include ministry to family members, opportunities to express God's love at work or school, etc.

ACTIVITY 6 (8-10 min.)

Praying for One Another

Form groups of three or four. Suggest that each person in the group share what he or she wants God to do in his or her life during the remainder of this study. Then group members close by praying for one another.

Reflect and look ahead

By the end of the session, do you feel each participant was willing to claim that he or she was called to minister? If so, you achieved your session goal. If not, it doesn't mean you failed. Some people may take longer than others.

This was probably a familiar concept for many of your group members, but the session may have still been significant for them as they shared their ideas about ministry, their frustrations, and what they hope God will do for them in the coming weeks. Did you sense a growing excitement and anticipation about what God is wanting to do in the group and in your church?

Were misconceptions about ministry expressed? Frustrations? Hopes? Keep these in mind as you prepare for future sessions.

SESSION 2

WASHING DIRTY FEET

> **SESSION GOAL**
> *To help each participant realize that God calls us to minister to all kinds of needs, not just spiritual needs.*

Materials and advance preparation needed
1. Chalkboard or newsprint and marker
2. Bibles

ACTIVITY 1 (5 min.)

Do I Really Have a Ministry?

One person who enrolled in a group study of lay ministry gave this reason for wanting to explore the topic further: "I have not been effective as a soul winner, and that leaves me wondering if I really have a ministry." Read that statement to your group; then ask, **"Have any of you ever had similar feelings?"**

You might expand the statement to include other activities widely recognized as ministry because they address spiritual needs—teaching, preaching, counseling, leading worship, and so on. The goal of this activity is to encourage any group members who feel that ministry is limited primarily to meeting spiritual needs to express whatever frustrations that view may have caused them.

ACTIVITY 2 (10-20 min.)

Two Motivations for Ministry

Ask for a volunteer to read the story in chapter 2 under the heading "What needs does love care about?" After the story is read, write the following heading and column headings across the top of your chalkboard or newsprint:

MINISTRY MOTIVATED BY:

Law	Love

Ask group members first to describe what adjectives they would use to describe ministry motivated by law. Likely answers include "judgmental," "self-righteous," "conditional," "guilt-motivated," "fear-motivated," etc. Then ask what ministry motivated by love might look like. Likely answers include "unconditional," "sensitive," "accepting," etc.

As group members answer, invite them to explain briefly. Without putting anyone on the spot, give opportunity for people's comments to expand into describing their own experiences. It is likely that group members have had similar experience in struggling with legalistic motivations for ministry, and it can be healing and empowering for them to discover that they are on the same spiritual journey.

In summary, point out the relationship between love and whole-person ministry. While law-motivated ministry can narrowly define what is ministry (what needs we are obligated to respond to) and what is not, it is the nature of love to respond to all kinds of needs, not to address spiritual needs and ignore all other kinds of needs.

ACTIVITY 3 (10-12 min.)

The Needs Love Touches

Ask for four volunteers to read the following Scripture passages. Briefly introduce the reading of each passage as described and follow each reading with the questions shown.

1. **"This passage in Luke 4 is sometimes called Jesus' 'inaugural address' because He made this statement at the beginning of His public ministry as an announcement of His mission."** (Read Luke 4:14-21.)
"What kinds of needs did Jesus say God's Spirit had sent Him to meet?"

2. **"Toward the end of Jesus' ministry, John the Baptist sent two of his disciples to Jesus to ask if He was in fact the Messiah. Rather than answer yes or no, Jesus listed certain activities, implying that these activities proved He was the Messiah."** (Read Matt. 11:2-5.)

"What kinds of ministry did Jesus feel demonstrated His Messiahship? What kinds of needs had been met? (Were spiritual needs the only ones He listed?)"

3. **"Jesus may have told this following parable just to make sure there was no room for doubt among any of His listeners that we too are to minister to the needs of the whole person just as He did."** (Read Matt. 25:31-46.)

"Did Jesus make ministry to needs other than spiritual needs optional for His followers, or does He expect it of all of us?"

4. **"Finally, one more reminder that love cannnot say yes to spiritual needs but say no to other kinds of needs."** (Read 1 John 3:17.)

"So, if we minister to spiritual needs only but don't minister to other needs, are we carrying out Christ's mission? If we minister to social needs only but don't minister to spiritual needs, are we carrying out Christ's mission? (No, faithfulness to Christ's mission demands that we respond compassionately to the needs of the total person, both spiritual and social.)"

ACTIVITY 4 (5-8 min.)

Love in Action

Ask one or two volunteers to read the story of Steve and Cyndi Lamb from chapter 2, which appears under the subheading "Behold, how they love." If you know of a similar story that has taken place in your church or community, an alternative would be to invite a group member to share it with the group. An important element in the Lamb story is that the church's outpouring of compassion led to evangelism, simply because someone was so impressed at seeing such love in action that she was motivated to investigate what was behind it. If you use a story from your own community, it would be good to choose one that also shows how ministry to nonspiritual needs can result in spiritual needs being met.

ACTIVITY 5 (6-8 min.)

A Liberating Call

As preparation for this activity, study the section of the chapter under the subheading "A liberating call" and be prepared to present the content of this section in a three- to four-minute minilecture. After explaining the concepts, say

* **"Think back to the story of the Lambs [or the story you used in its place]. What were some of the different gifts or abilities people used in ministering to this family?"**

* **"Did all of these gifts or abilities minister directly to spiritual needs? How might this story have unfolded differently if the only needs ministered to had been the Lambs' [or the person in your story] spiritual needs?"**

The point, of course, is that for the world to see God's love fully expressed, we must respond in love to the needs of the whole person—and when we do, people will take notice.

Write the word "MINISTRY" across the top of your chalkboard or newsprint, then draw a wheel with six or eight spokes. Label one spoke "spiritual needs." Explain: **"One reason some people find it so difficult to discover their ministry is that they have gotten the idea that this [the "spiritual needs" spoke] is all there is to ministry. Then if their particular gifts for ministry don't fit here, they get frustrated and conclude that they don't have a ministry. In reality, the problem is that their ministry lies in one or more of these other areas, but they don't know these areas involve ministry just as much as the spiritual spoke does."** Label some of the other spokes with such labels as "financial needs," "practical needs," "emotional needs," etc.

"Everyone here has a God-given ability to minister to one or more of these kinds of needs, and each of your ministries is needed if the church is to fulfill all of Christ's mission in our community."

ACTIVITY 6 (5-10 min.)

Washing Feet—Past and Future

Form groups of three or four and ask each person to share in the group (1) one way God has used him to meet a need in another person's life and (2) one way he will try to "wash dirty feet" during the coming week. This could be anything from volunteering with a food pantry to visiting a nursing home to writing an encouraging note. Next week, each person should come prepared to report on how the "foot washing" experience went. After all have shared, have the small groups close by members praying for one another's ministries.

Reflect and look ahead

Did your group include some with a spiritual-needs-only (or primarily so) view of ministry? If so, has this caused them any frustration?

Did group members see how love inevitably leads to whole-person ministry? Were they able to visualize what whole-person ministry might look like?

If you had some spiritual-needs-only people in your group, did they find the concept of whole-person ministry threatening or liberating? Were any able to identify other areas where they might have ministry gifts?

How easy or difficult was it for people to name ways God had used them in other people's lives?

Were any concerns expressed in this session that you think deserve particular attention in the coming weeks?

SESSION 3

THE EMPTY SANCTUARY

SESSION GOAL
To help participants realize that most ministry takes place, not when the church is gathered, but when the church is scattered—and to be more aware of ways they are ministering or could be ministering when the church is scattered.

Materials and advance preparation needed
1. Chalkboard or newsprint and marker
2. Paper and pencils for each participant
3. Bible

ACTIVITY 1 (8-12 min.)

Survey of Ministries
    Ask your group, **"What are some of the ministries of this local church fellowship?"** As answers are called out, list them on a chalkboard or newsprint. Continue for five or six minutes or until the answers stop coming, whichever comes first.
    Affirm the importance of all these ministries, and note the number and variety of these ministries.
    Next, lead the group through your list and ask them to indicate which of the listed ministries take place when the church is gathered (mark these G) and which take place when the church is scattered (mark these S). For example, worship services would be marked G; nursing home visitation would be marked S. Any ministries that take place in both settings can be marked GS.
    When the group has gone through the whole list, ask if

there seem to be more *G's* or more *S's*.

If your group has listed more *G's*, observe, **"When we think about the ministries of our fellowship, it is easiest to think of the ministries of the church gathered. They tend to be the most visible. But in reality, most of the ministry of this fellowship takes place during the week when the congregation is scattered."** Go on to give examples of ways members of the fellowship minister through the week—parents ministering to their children, spouses ministering to each other, nurses ministering to their patients, teachers meeting the needs of their students, people who do volunteer work with community organizations, etc. (Read chapters 3 and 4 of the text for possible examples.)

Point out that sometimes we think of the church primarily as an organization, so we include only official ministry programs when we list the ministries of the church. But since the church is a body of believers, the ministries of the church include the ministries of all the members of that body. And most of this ministry takes place, not when the church is gathered, but when the church is scattered.

Why is this important? Because so long as we think of ministry as something that only takes place "at the church" or through a church program, we will fail to recognize that much of what we are doing every day is, or can be, ministry. This misconception can even keep people from discovering their calls. Because they do not recognize that certain activities can be ministry, they may not realize that a God-given desire to serve in such ways is actually a call to ministry.

ACTIVITY 2 (6-8 min.)

Why Does the Church Gather?

Ask for a volunteer to read the section of chapter 3 headed "Why does the church gather?"

Then say, **"The church gathers for a number of reasons. What are some of those reasons?"** Affirm the answers people give. Note that some of the reasons we gather, such as worshiping God, are ends in themselves. We do not do them as a means to do something else. Being community has value in and of itself. In these areas, the church is different from the sales team described in the passage just read.

But the church is similar to the sales team in the area of mission. Continue to ask questions and invite response until you feel the group has grasped the meaning of the sales team analogy—that a major reason the church gathers is to prepare and equip for its ministry as the church scattered. If the church's gathering does not result in effective ministry of the church scattered during the week, our gathering has failed to meet one of its major purposes.

ACTIVITY 3 (6-8 min.)

Where Ministry Happens

Ask for a volunteer to read Rom. 12:4-8, pausing each time he or she comes to the name of one of the spiritual gifts, allowing you time to write the name of the gift on your chalkboard or newsprint. Make your list in a column on the left side. Then next to your list make a chart as shown.

	Church gathered	Church scattered
Prophesying		
Serving		
Teaching		
Encouraging		
Giving		
Leadership		
Showing mercy		

Go through the list, gift by gift. Talk briefly about what each gift is. Don't get hung up on precise definitions; the Bible does not define the gifts precisely. Then ask, **"Is this a gift that is exercised when the church is gathered or when the church is scattered?"** Put an X in the appropriate spaces. Most, probably all, of the gifts can be excercised in either setting, either with a group or one-on-one. If the gift is used more in one setting than in the other (for example, prophesying is usually done in a group; showing mercy usually one-on-one), circle the X in that column.

This activity has two purposes. First, it is to reinforce the idea that ministry takes place just as truly when the church is scattered as when it is gathered. Second, and you will need to point this out, it shows that some people's gifts are most often used one-on-one, not in groups. If they think of ministry mainly in terms of gatherings, they may have trouble finding their spiritual gifts or feel they are not gifted. Therefore, when someone is trying to identify call, it is crucial to consider the ministries of the church scattered.

ACTIVITY 4 (6-8 min.)

From Sanctuary to Tavern
    Read, or call on one of your better readers to read, the Jim Couchenour story found at the beginning of the chapter. Then say, **"Jim had been a deeply committed member of Columbiana Church of the Nazarene for 28 years; yet he had been unaware of the tremendous human need in the community right around the church. Is it possible that we in our church may have overlooked some of the most pressing human needs right in our own community?"**

ACTIVITY 5 (2-6 min.)

Opportunities for Ministry
    Pass out paper and pencils to each person. Ask group members to turn their papers so that the long side is up and make four columns. They should label these columns "WORLD," "COMMUNITY," "FAMILY," and "CHURCH," and draw a line just under the headings across the page. Now have them turn their papers so that those headings are on the left edge of the paper, and draw a line dividing the paper into two vertical columns. Have them head the left column "NEEDS." For now, leave the second column blank. The chart should look like this.

	NEEDS	
Church		
Family		
Community		
World		

Give group members two minutes to list needs they are aware of in each of the four categories—church, family, community, world. These can include both needs to which they are ministering, as well as needs to which they are not ministering.

After two minutes, have the group members add the heading "POSSIBLE RESPONSES" to the second column; then take a couple of minutes to reflect on how they might respond to some of these needs if they felt so led.

If time is running short, skip the chart-making, and simply ask people to think of one way they are regularly ministering to a need in their church, family, community, or world, and one need to which they wonder if God might be wanting them to minister. They will share these in the next activity. Try to save at least 6 minutes for the final activity.

ACTIVITY 6 (6-10 min.)

Considering Our Responses

Form groups of three or four and give the following instructions: **"Begin by reporting briefly on the act of foot washing you committed to do at the end of the last session. What did you do? How did it go?**

"After that, name one need from your list in the last activity to which you are already regularly ministering. Then name one need to which you feel God may be wanting you to respond. Once everyone has shared, close by praying for one another, both about your continuing ministries and for guidance about future ministries."

Reflect and look ahead

Each session so far has expanded the definition of ministry. Are your group members seeing that ministry is something every Christian does? That it can be in response to any kind of need? And that it can happen in any setting? Are they beginning to see that most ministry is not organizationally related to the church, but that it happens wherever Christians respond in love to anyone?

These are all simple concepts, but for those to whom they are new, they can be life changing. The next session will focus on how ordinary work can be transformed into ministry.

SESSION 4

THE MYTH OF SECULAR WORK

SESSION GOAL
To help participants understand the relationship between work and ministry and to learn how they can minister more effectively through their work.

Materials and advance preparation needed

1. Tools representing various kinds of work, such as a hammer, overalls, dish towel, Bible commentary, etc. Arrange these in a display at the front of the room before the session.
2. Chalkboard or newsprint with marker
3. Bibles, including several each of King James Version and contemporary translations.

ACTIVITY 1

Secular Jobs (3-4 min.)

Open your session something like this: **"Today we're going to be talking about ministering through our work. We won't be talking primarily about ministry professionals like church staff or employees of Christian ministry organizations, though they may learn something useful. Rather, we're going to be talking about how those of us who work in schools, homes, offices, stores, or factories can minister through our jobs.**

"How many here regularly do some kind of secular work—either paid or unpaid? Would you raise your hands?

"OK. Since so many of you do secular work, it shouldn't be too hard for us to come up with a defini-

tion of *secular*. **What does *secular* mean?"** (Optional: Jot answers on a chalkboard or newsprint.)

Since most dictionaries define *secular* by telling what it is *not* (for example, "not religious or related to the church"), you'll probably want to ask, **"What words are opposites of *secular*?"** (Possible answers: religious, sacred, holy.)

ACTIVITY 2

Ministry Tools (1-2 min.)

Draw attention to the tools you've displayed in the front of the room. Ask, **"Which of these are ministry tools? Why?"** Don't try to reach a consensus or guide people to the right answer just yet. The purpose of this activity is simply to define the question. The next activity will move you toward an answer.

ACTIVITY 3

Secular Jobs Don't Have to Be (8-10 min.)

Continue by saying, **"Most of us (except perhaps those who 'cheated' and read the chapter before class) see ourselves as working in secular jobs. Our jobs don't seem particularly religious, holy, or sacred. But it doesn't have to be that way. Sometimes simply by viewing through new eyes what we are already doing, we can see our jobs as ministries. Some of us may need to approach our work in new ways to turn our jobs into ministries. A few may even need to consider changing jobs if we determine that God cannot be glorified through our present jobs. But all of us can minister through our work, just as truly as the person on staff with a church or Christian ministry organization.**

"Jan Lundy's story is an example of how a job that is usually considered secular can be approached as a ministry."

Ask for a volunteer to read the Jan Lundy story found at the beginning of chapter 4. It ends at the first subheading.

After the story is read, ask the group to list the ways Jan

ministers through Precision Histology. List answers on your chalkboard or newsprint.

Once the list is complete, ask:

* **"Which of these ministries is Jan able to do because she manages her own business and can therefore set policy?"** As people indicate items from the list, mark them with an *M* for "manager." (Possible answers: Offer employment and job training to those with limited economic opportunities; provide on-site child care to employees, both meeting an economic need and strengthening family relationships; include employees' families in social events; prepare slides without charge for nonprofit clinics.)

* **"Which of these ministries could she do even if she had no policy-making authority?"** Mark these with an *E* to indicate that every employee can do these. (Possible answers: Show God's love and share her faith with coworkers; consistently do work of the highest quality as a service to the patients to insure each one gets the best possible diagnosis.)

* **"What does our analysis suggest about the ministry potential of the owner/manager of a business?"** (Such a person is in a position to build the business completely on biblical principles and to base all company policies on the goal of making the entire business a ministry.)

* **"What does it say about the possibility of ministering as an employee?"** (Even people who have little or no authority to influence company policies can approach their jobs as ministries.)

ACTIVITY 4

Secular or Sacred? (6-10 min.)

Ask for a volunteer to read 1 Cor. 10:31.

Ask for another volunteer to read the section of chapter 4 headed "Secular or sacred?"

Then say, **"The key to understanding how our work can also be ministry is found in understanding the basic nature of ministry. In earlier chapters, ministry has been defined as 'doing love' and 'loving people**

like Jesus would.' Those are great definitions focusing on the motive behind ministry. But when it comes to understanding what kinds of activities can be ministry, a brief Greek word study may shed some light.

"When we see the words *minister* or *ministry* in the New Testament, particularly in the King James Version, the Greek word being translated is usually some form of the word *diakonia.* To get an idea of what *diakonia* really means, we're going to compare some verses where this word is translated 'minister' or 'ministry' in the King James Version with those same verses in modern translations. By listening to both versions, see if you can figure out how the word *diakonia* is translated in the modern versions."

Now ask for volunteers to look up and read the following passages, first in the King James, then in a modern translation. If you have time, you might ask for the reading of a second modern translation. The words found in modern translations follow the references. Jot these down on your chalkboard or newsprint as people identify them.

Matt. 20:26, 28 (servant, serve)
Acts 13:5 (assistant, helper)
1 Pet. 4:10 (serve)
Eph. 4:12 (service, ministry. Note: RSV and NRSV retain the word *ministry* in this verse.)

Ask, **"So what does *diakonia* mean?"** (Service.) To minister is simply to serve. Once we understand this, we have the key to understanding how we can minister through our work.

ACTIVITY 5

What Makes a Job a Ministry? (8-12 min.)

Now ask for a volunteer to read the section of the chapter headed "Test No. 1: Does your work meet needs?" As the person is reading, write on the chalkboard or newsprint (or have it written on newsprint before the session): "What need do you meet through your work?"

Next ask for a volunteer to read the next section, "Test No. 2: Do you have a servant spirit?" and for another to read the first three paragraphs only under "Who is it you're serving?" As these are being read, write on the board or news-print, "What serves or could serve to remind you daily who it is you're serving?"

Finally, ask someone to read the section of the chapter headed, "Beyond the job description." As it is being read, write the question "What opportunities does your work give you to respond to needs (minister) beyond what your work requires you to do?"

If you feel it is needed, you can quickly summarize the points made in the portions of the chapter that have been read aloud.

ACTIVITY 6

Sharing and Prayer (6-10 min.)

Form groups of three or four. Have each person share with his group answers to the three questions you have writ-ten on the chalkboard or newsprint. After each person in the group has answered all the questions, each group should close with prayer. Suggest that each person pray aloud for the ministry of the person on his left.

Reflect and look ahead

Were the ideas in this session new to a lot of your group? Did you feel they were able to apply these principles to their own work situations?

One of the most difficult principles for some employed people to apply is identifying who it is they are serving by their work. It is easy to see that they are helping their employers. It is easy to see they are providing for their fami-lies. But it may be less obvious who benefits from the prod-ucts or services the business exists to provide. Was this con-cept clear to your group members?

Serious reflection on this week's topic will eventually lead some Christians to question whether they are in the job that gives them the greatest opportunity for ministry. That is a great question! Next week's session on how to recognize what kind of ministry God is calling you to will help your group members answer it.

SESSION 5
DISCOVERING YOUR CALL

Session goal
To help participants identify their spiritual gifts and discern their calls to ministry.

Materials and advance preparation needed

1. Materials for making name tags (for example, index cards, colored markers, tape, and safety pins; or construction paper, yarn, scissors, and crayons). These should not be self-adhesive name tags. They will need to be taken off and put back on.
2. A gift-wrapped box and a telephone (does not need to be connected). Before the session, display these on a table at the front of the room.
3. Bibles
4. Chalkboard or newsprint and marker
5. Pens or pencils and paper

ACTIVITY 1

Name Tags (2 min.)
Have materials for making name tags on a table at the doorway where people enter your meeting room, and ask each one to make a name tag before taking a seat.

ACTIVITY 2

Introduction (2 min.)
Briefly review the key truths you have studied in the previous four sessions; then introduce this week's topic. Point out that in each of the previous four sessions you have been broadening the definition of ministry. Show how you have done that in each session. The purpose of this session,

though, is to help each participant begin to focus on what specific part of God's mission in the world he or she is called to be involved in. To do that, you will be looking at two important biblical concepts—gifts and call. One way to think of it is that you will be exploring how to "unwrap your gifts" (point out the gift-wrapped box) and how to hear and answer the call (point out the telephone).

ACTIVITY 3

How Gifts and Call Emerge (3-5 min.)

Ask, **"How can we know what our spiritual gifts are?"** After participants have had a chance to comment, ask a volunteer to read the first section of chapter 5 up to the first subhead.

Before going on, make sure the group understands that a spiritual gift is visible only when it is in use. You cannot discover your gift first, then use it. Rather, you have to begin to minister, and in the process of ministering, your gift emerges —you and others see it at work.

Say, **"In a moment you'll form small groups and try to name each other's spiritual gifts; but before you do that, I want to point out two common hindrances to discovering spiritual gifts—the confusion between gifts and talents, and being overly concerned with using technically correct labels for spiritual gifts."** Both of these are explained in the section of chapter 5 headed "Congratulations! You're gifted!" Rather than asking someone to read that section, explain these two points briefly (1-2 minutes) in your own words.

ACTIVITY 4

Calling Forth Gifts (8-12 min.)

Form groups of four. One person will pass his name tag around the group, and each of the other persons will write on the name tag the name of a spiritual gift he has seen at work through that person's life, and briefly comment on how he has seen this gift at work. Of course, if anyone does not know the person well enough to name a gift, it is fine to pass. Repeat this process with each of the other three name tags.

ACTIVITY 5

What Is Call? (3-5 min.)
Ask someone to read 1 Cor. 12:4-6.
Point out that verse 4 mentions the different gifts God has given each of us, and verse 5 mentions the different kinds of ministries or service to which God calls each of us.
    * Ask, **"Do all the people who have the same gift also have the same kind of ministry?"** Have those who respond explain their answers. (No, they don't. For example, one person with the gift of teaching may be a pastor, another a Sunday School teacher, another a counselor, another a writer. Each gift can be used in many different kinds of ministries.)
    Explain that for the purposes of this study, we are using the word "call" to mean the ministry or kind of ministry in which God is leading a person to use his spiritual gifts. To this point in the session you have focused mostly on gifts. Now you're going to shift your focus to discovering call.

ACTIVITY 6

Discovering Call (10-12 min.)
    Write the following questions on your chalkboard or newsprint. Or, you can have them written on newsprint or poster board before the session.
    1. Where do you mourn with Jesus for the pain in the world?
    2. What would give you joy in that painful situation?
    3. If you had unlimited resources, what would you dream of doing in response to this need?
    4. What would you have to risk or give up to pursue this dream?
    Explain that both pain (question 1) and joy (question 2) are important clues to call. You might mention an example such as Dillard Taylor, who started a support group for unemployed people after he experienced unemployment, or someone your group members would know. You might tie pain and joy together by saying that call is often found **"where the world's deep pain and your deep joy intersect."**
    Point out that question 3 is partly a restatement of ques-

tion 2, but it asks us to be specific and dream big. Question 4 asks us to consider the cost of obeying call.

In a moment you're going to ask the group to take five minutes to reflect silently and prayerfully on these questions in relation to their own calls. But before you do that, point out to the group that discovering call is seldom easy and may take place over a period of weeks, months, or even years. While some of them may leave this session with clear answers to all the "call" questions, others may search for months before finding answers. The purpose of this activity is not to produce instant answers for everyone, but rather to help them understand the process by which they can work at discerning call.

Check to see if there are any questions; then ask the group to enter into five minutes of silent reflection on the questions. Some may find it helpful to jot down their answers onto paper.

At the end of five minutes, suggest that those who need more time to consider their answers should write down the four questions and take them home. In the next session, you will be doing more work with these same four questions.

Also encourage everyone to read carefully chapter 5 of the text in preparation for the next session, giving special attention to the last two sections of the chapter, which discuss team ministry.

ACTIVITY 7

Sharing and Prayer (8-15 min.)

Have participants once again form their groups of four. Invite those who wish to do so to share with the others in the group their answers to the four questions. Keep an eye on the clock, and limit each person's sharing to allow others time to share.

Close the session with each person's praying for the one on his right in response to what has been shared.

Reflect and look ahead

While each of the first four sessions were designed to broaden participants' understanding of ministry, this session seeks to help each person focus on where his or her ministry fits into the total ministry of the body. This session therefore has a stronger element of personal application than the others.

Do you feel your group members are understanding what spiritual gifts are and how to identify theirs? Do they understand what a call is and how to clarify what God is calling them to do during this period of their lives?

While each of the first four sesssions stand alone pretty well, sessions 5 and 6 are closely related. Session 6, in fact, is really an extension of session 5, though it introduces a new element: once you have discovered call, it is important to pursue that call—not alone, but together with others God has called to the same ministry.

Now may be an important time for you to check in with your pastor, reporting on the responses of group members and thinking together about what kind of follow-through may be called for after the final session of the study. How can the church support people in living out their new understandings of ministry and call?

SESSION 6

A QUIET REVOLUTION

> **SESSION GOAL**
> *To help participants see the importance of team ministry and understand how to begin forming a ministry team.*

Materials and advance preparation needed

1. Before the session, have written on newsprint or poster board the four "call" questions used in the last session (Activity 6).
2. Before the session, prepare, or ask a group member to prepare, a three-minute summary of the section of this chapter headed "A revolution in Oklahoma." This should *not* include the six examples of actual ministry teams at the end of that section. This summary should focus on (1) how the need to form ministry teams arose and (2) how the teams were formed.

ACTIVITY 1

Introducing Ministry Teams (10-12 min.)

Open with a three-minute summary of why and how ministry teams were formed at Bethany First Church of the Nazarene. (See "Materials and advance preparation needed," No. 2.) This can be done either by you or by someone to whom you assign this in advance.

Follow this by asking six volunteers each to read one of the six examples of specific ministries at the end of the section of the chapter headed "A Revolution in Oklahoma."

You might give participants a chance to respond to the ministry team concept. What advantages does it have? What risks does it involve?

ACTIVITY 2

Sounding Call (10-15 min.)

Draw the group's attention to the four "call" questions you introduced last week in Activity 6. While people respond-ed to these in small groups, the larger group has not yet heard people's responses to these questions (unless your group is so small you did not subdivide into groups last week). You may also have some present in this session who were not present at the last session.

Quickly review the questions; then give participants a chance to share their sense of call—where the world's deep pain and their deep joy intersect—as well as their dream of how they would like to respond to that need. How much time each person can take will depend on the size of your group.

During this activity as people share from the deepest places within their spirits, you will be on holy ground. This is not the time to critique or ask someone to defend a sense of call. This is a time to listen with profound respect. Affirm as you are able.

List on your chalkboard or newsprint each call described. For example, "ministry to abused children," "outreach to young adults," "church planting," etc.

ACTIVITY 3

Forming Ministry Teams (15-20 min.)

Explain that one way to form ministry teams is to invite people to "sound their calls," describing what ministries they believe God is calling them to do. This is what you have just done.

Then people with similar calls can get together to ex-plore forming a team. Often as someone hears another describe a call, he or she is drawn to join that ministry.

Today you will role-play the formation of ministry teams. Ask those who named each of the circled calls to stand and go to various parts of the room. Then ask everyone else pres-ent to choose which of those ministries he or she is most interested in and to join the person who sounded that call. If someone is left alone (no one responds to that call), ask that person to choose another group to join.

Now each group is to role-play an organizational meeting of the ministry team. Within the time allowed, they are to see how far they can get in making the following plans:

1. What will the ministry team try to accomplish? (The group may either settle on one or two goals or may come up with a number of possibilities.)

2. Based on the interests, experience, and spiritual gifts each person brings to the group, what might be each person's position on the team? What role could each play?

Obviously this task cannot be completed in 10 to 15 minutes, but this is long enough to get people to start thinking in terms of team ministry.

ACTIVITY 4

Reporting (6-10 min.)

Ask a spokesperson from each group to report on what goals the group set and to name some of the roles people would fill in the ministry team.

After the reporting, acknowledge that what you have just done was a role play. Many of the participants may not actually be called to the ministry teams they just met with. Yet also point out that some ministry teams have in fact been started with such a role-play activity and that there may be a group or two who will want to continue meeting on their own after the study is finished to actually organize a new ministry. Encourage any who have such an interest to follow through, and offer any personal practical support you wish to make available.

ACTIVITY 5

The Quiet Revolution (2-5 min.)

Read the Elton Trueblood quote that appears just before the beginning of chapter 6. Then ask the group to imagine: **"What would happen in our church if each of the ministry teams we just envisioned became a reality? What if not just the laypeople in this room, but every layperson in this church, identified a personal call to ministry and committed himself or herself wholeheartedly to obeying that call in cooperation with other believers?**

**What would happen to this church? What kind of impact
would this church make on this community?"**
If time permits, you can invite responses.

ACTIVITY 6

Closing Prayer (2-5 min.)
Ask the whole group to stand, form a circle, and hold
hands. As your final act together in this study, invite people to
pray conversationally as they wish, and name a person to close
the prayer.

Reflect and look ahead
What happened in this session is a good clue to how much
of an impact the study made on the participants. If they have
been challenged by what they have been learning, this session
was probably a powerful time of sounding call, envisioning
greater possibilities for ministry, and expressing gratitude to
God. If they have not been challenged by the sessions, this final
session may have seemed a bit hollow, with little excitement.

Do you have people in the group who are now ready to
move out into ministry? Does the church need to provide practical support in forming ministry teams? Are there other ways
the church should follow up this study to empower participants
to say yes to God's calls in their lives?

These are critical questions. Whether this study serves as a
catalyst to empower its participants to be more effective in
ministry may depend more on what happens next than on
what has happened so far.

You may also want to consider whether this study needs to
be offered again in the congregation. Has enough enthusiasm
been generated among those participating that others would
want to take part if it were repeated?

Finally, if this study has been done in a relatively small
group and significant ministry initiatives are emerging from the
group, you may want to arrange a time that a few of the participants could report to the entire congregation on what they
are learning about ministry and what God seems to be saying
to them about call. This is one way to extend the impact of the
study beyond those who actually attend the sessions to make it
a catalyst for congregational renewal.